SAP Certified Application Associate –

SAP Hybris Sales Cloud

By

J. Jacobs & N. Kaur

Copyright Notice

Contents

Before you Start..

Before you start here are some Key features of the *SAP Certified Application Consultant – SAP Hybris Sales Cloud* certification test.

This certification path will validate your capability as a well-trained consultant prepared to help your client or employer manage and execute key business processes.

This certificate proves that the candidate has the required understanding within this consultant profile, and can implement this knowledge practically in projects under guidance of an experienced consultant.

✓ Associate Certifications are targeting profiles with 1 - 3 years of knowledge and experience. The primary source of knowledge and skills is based on the corresponding training material.

✓ The exam is Computer based and you have three Hours to answer 80 Questions.

✓ The Questions are (mostly) multiple choice type and there is NO penalty for an incorrect answer.

✓ Some of the Questions have more than one correct answer. You must get ALL the options correct for you to be awarded points.

✓ For questions with a single answer, the answers will have a button next to them. You will be able to select only one button.

✓ For questions with multiple answers, the answers will have a 'tick box' next to them. This allows you to select multiple answers.

✓ You are not allowed to use any reference materials during the certification test (no access to online documentation or to any SAP system).

✓ The Official Pass percentage is 65%. (This can vary slightly for your exam)

✓ In this book, unless otherwise stated, there is only one correct answer.

Lead and Opportunity Management

1.   **Which of the following are the benefits of Lead Management?**

      Note: There are 2 correct answers to this question.

      a. Lengthened sales cycles
      b. Forecast based on multiple dimensions
      c. Improved sales efficiency
      d. Streamlined sales process

      Answer: c, d

      Explanation:

      Lead Management:

      Description:
      - Manages potential business opportunities with automated tools to qualify, score, route, and nurture in order to convert them into sales
      - Automatically age leads and notifies when leads are not addressed

      Key Differentiators:
      - Manages end to end process of deal management
      - Uses predictive analytics to score and suggest potential deals

      Benefits:
      - Improved sales efficiency
      - Streamlined sales process
      - High potential Leads
      - Shortened sales cycles

      Sales cycles are shortened through lead management, and Forecast based on multiple dimensions is not a benefit of Lead Management.

2.   **Which of the following statement(s) is/are true regarding Lead Status?**

      Please choose the correct answer.

      a. You can delete pre-delivered statuses
      b. You can deactivate pre-delivered statuses
      c. Both a and b
      d. None of the above

      Answer: b

Explanation:

Lead Status:

- Maintains the statuses (Open, Qualified, Accepted, Declined, In Approval) of your leads and creates new lead statuses, if desired.

- The status converted is the logical end of the status chain. You cannot assign any conversion action to this status and you cannot assign it to a lead manually, but you can search for it. Also, you can deactivate pre-delivered statuses, but you cannot delete them.

- User status is exposed on the lead header and qualified leads can be accepted or declined.

3.   **Which of the following is NOT a standard Lead qualification level?**
      Please choose the correct answer.

   a. Cold
   b. Hot
   c. Warm
   d. Dark

Answer: d

Explanation:

Lead Qualification:

Lead qualification level represents the likelihood for the lead to be converted to a real opportunity.

Standard qualification levels are cold, warm and hot. New levels can be created during configuration. 'Dark' is not a standard Lead qualification level.

Lead qualification level can be manually maintained or automatically updated via surveys, lead attributes are available for setting up conditions to assign surveys.

4. **Which of the following statement(s) is/are true regarding Lead Conversion?**

Please choose the correct answer.

a. The conversion of a lead into an opportunity or account and contact is the final stage of a lead lifecycle
b. A lead can be converted to only one opportunity
c. The link between an opportunity and its lead is maintained to track effectiveness of the demand generation process
d. Only a and c
e. None of the above

Answer: d

Explanation:

Lead Conversion:

- The conversion of a lead into an opportunity or account and contact is the final stage of a lead lifecycle

- The link between an opportunity and its lead is maintained to track effectiveness of the demand generation process

- A lead is converted into one or more opportunities, the limit is defined in configuration

5. **Which of the following are the benefits of Activity Management?**

Note: There are 2 correct answers to this question.

a. Calendar management across multiple channels
b. Creation of multiple activities at one Shot
c. Incremental revenue growth
d. Improved value proposition through partner value add

Answer: a, b

Explanation:

Activity Management:

Description:
- View, plan and create activities to manage customer interactions during customer relationship lifecycle across different devices.

Key Differentiators:
- Receive recommended activities and best content for each buying stage
- Create consistent engagement models

Benefits:
- Calendar management across multiple Channels
- Creation of multiple activities at one Shot
- Easy creation of follow-up documents
- Quick Appointment creation via iPad

Incremental revenue growth and improved value proposition through partner value add are not the benefits of Activity Management.

6. **Which of the following are the benefits of Mobility?**

Note: There are 2 correct answers to this question.

a. Collaboration support
b. Superior UI/UX
c. Forecast any time on any device
d. Ability to leverage existing analytics to manage against forecast in real time

Answer: a, b

Explanation:

Mobility:

Description:
- Support for iPhone, iPad, Blackberry, and Android devices means you'll have more meaningful customer interactions anytime, anywhere

Key Differentiators:
- The most superior UI/UX in the market
- Online and Offline capabilities

Benefits:
- Mobile offline capabilities
- Mobile access included in license
- Collaboration support
- Superior UI/UX

Forecast any time on any device and ability to leverage existing analytics to manage against forecast in real time are not the benefits of Mobility.

7. **Which of the following statement(s) is/are true regarding SAP Hybris Cloud for Sales?**

Please choose the correct answer.

a. Platform is Real-time, scalable, powered by SAP HANA
b. Has Pre-built integration to SAP ERP & CRM, SAP JAM
c. Has Partners like InsideView, D&B 360, Xactly & more
d. Only a and b
e. a, b, and c

Answer: e

Explanation:

Highlights of SAP Hybris Cloud for Sales are given below:

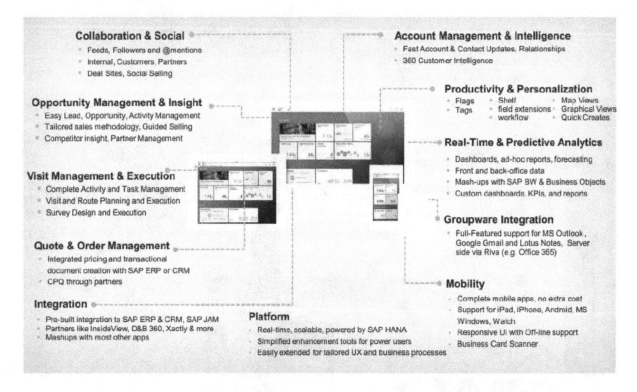

8.   **Which of the following are the benefits of Partner Channel Management?**

Note: There are 2 correct answers to this question.

a. Calendar management across multiple channels
b. Creation of multiple activities at one Shot
c. Incremental revenue growth
d. Improved sales coverage through extended market reach

Answer: c, d

Explanation:

Partner Channel Management:

Description:

- Effectively drive revenue through your partner channels with partner data management, lead routing, collaborative opportunity management, and partner program management.

Key Differentiators:

- Intuitive and tailorable user experience for partner users.
- Simplified program management.

Benefits:

- Incremental revenue growth
- Improved value proposition through partner value add
- Improved sales coverage through extended market reach

Calendar management across multiple channels and Creation of multiple activities at one Shot are not the benefits of Partner Channel Management.

9.   **Which of the following are the key differentiators of Mobility?**

Note: There are 2 correct answers to this question.

a. The most superior UI/UX in the market
b. Offline and Online capabilities
c. Receive recommended activities and best content for each buying stage
d. Create consistent engagement models

Answer: a, b

Explanation:

Mobility:

Description:

- Support for iPhone, iPad, Blackberry, and Android devices means you'll have more meaningful customer interactions anytime, anywhere

Key Differentiators:
- The most superior UI/UX in the market
- Online and Offline capabilities

Receive recommended activities and best content for each buying stage and Create consistent engagement models are not the key differentiators.

Benefits:
- Mobile offline capabilities
- Mobile access included in license
- Collaboration support
- Superior UI/UX

10. **If a lead remains too long in a certain phase, then it is said to be aging. A notification of this type expires automatically in how many days after it has been created?**

Please choose the correct answer.

a. 12
b. 13
c. 14
d. 15

Answer: c

Explanation:

Lead Aging Notifications:

- If a lead remains too long in a certain phase, then it is said to be aging. In this case, the system notifies the manager of the sales representative who is responsible for the lead.

- This type of notification has priority high as a default.
- A notification of this type expires automatically 14 days after it has been created.
- You can define how the system behaves, modifying the business task for lead aging in fine- tuning

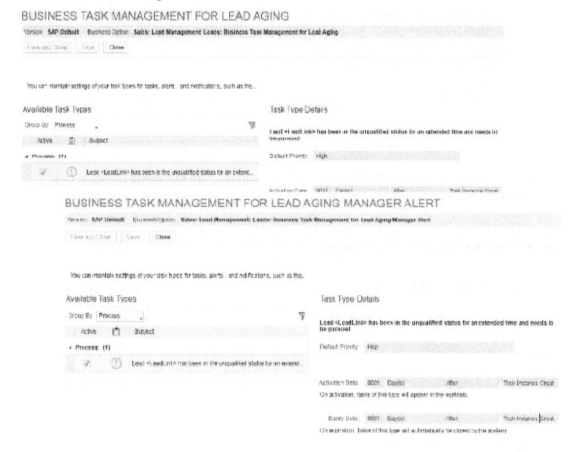

11.   **Which of the following are the features of Lead Management?**

Note: There are 3 correct answers to this question.

a. Lead routing
b. Standard analytical content
c. SAP Jam integration
d. Lead acceptance/rejection
e. Rule based party determination

Answer: a, b, d

Explanation:

Lead Management-Features:

- Lead routing
- Lead scoring using predictive engine
- Lead acceptance/rejection
- Lead nurturing
- Standard integration with lead generation systems (marketo, avention, etc.)
- Standard lead conversion analytics
- Workflow rule based notifications (tasks and emails)
- Lead-to-opportunity workflow
- Standard analytical content
- Business task to notify when leads are not actioned and escalations sent to management
- Leads on mobile devices

SAP Jam integration and Rule based party determination are not the features of Lead Management.

12. **Which of the following is NOT a Lead Status?**

Please choose the correct answer.

a. Qualified
b. Accepted
c. New
d. Declined

Answer: c

Explanation:

Lead Status:

- Maintains the statuses (Open, Qualified, Accepted, Declined, In Approval) of your leads and creates new lead statuses, if desired.
- The status converted is the logical end of the status chain. You cannot assign any conversion action to this status and you cannot assign it to a lead manually, but you can search for it. Also, you can deactivate pre-delivered statuses, but you cannot delete them.
- User status is exposed on the lead header and qualified leads can be accepted or declined.

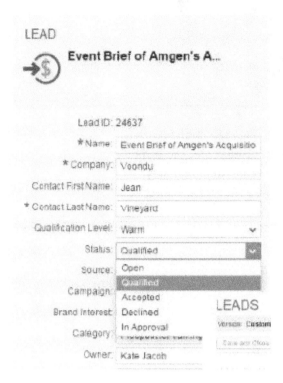

LEAD

Event Brief of Amgen's A...

Lead ID: 24637

*Name: Event Brief of Amgen's Acquisitio

*Company: Voondu

Contact First Name: Jean

*Contact Last Name: Vineyard

Qualification Level: Warm

Status: Qualified

Source: Open

Qualified

Campaign:

Accepted

Brand Interest: Declined

In Approval

Category:

Owner: Kate Jacob

LEADS

Version: Custom

13. **Which of the following is/are the feature(s) of Opportunity Management?**

Please choose the correct answer.

a. Rule based party determination
b. Pricing integration with ERP
c. SAP Jam integration
d. Only a and b
e. a, b, and c

Answer: e

Explanation:

Opportunity Management-Features:
- Opportunity capabilities such as create, view, update and delete
- Maintain Accounts, Contacts, Products, Marketing team, Activities & attachment
- Lead, Quotation and Order management integration
- Product Lists
- Revenue Split partners and Scheduling
- Pricing and Price Check (native SAP Hybris Cloud for Customer Pricing)
- Pricing integration with ERP (live call via order simulation)
- Rule based party determination
- Opportunity Pipeline Management

- Supports data sync with Microsoft Outlook
- Activity Timeline
- Influencer Map and Buying Center
- Notes and attachments
- Rule-based multi-step approval workflow
- Flexible notifications
- Output management, format templates, language selection in order
- Follow-on documents such as activities, visits, quotations and orders
- Trigger quotation/order request to SAP ERP, PDF order capability
- SAP Jam integration
- Change history
- Standard analytical content

14. **Which of the following statements are true regarding Revenue Splits and Revenue Schedule?**

   Note: There are 2 correct answers to this question.

   a. Revenue Split Partners can be selected from the Sales team of the opportunity
   b. Revenue Distribution can happen at Header level only
   c. Revenue Distribution can be based on Expected value of the opportunity only
   d. Revenue can be distributed monthly, quarterly or yearly

   Answer: a, d

   Explanation:

   Revenue Splits and Revenue Schedule:

- Revenue Split Partners can be selected from the Sales team of the opportunity.

- Revenue Distribution can happen at Header or at Item level. Distribution can be based on either Negotiated value or Expected value of the opportunity and can be distributed monthly, quarterly or yearly.

15. **Which of the following statement(s) is/are true regarding Influencer Map?**

Please choose the correct answer.

a. Influencer map allows you to visualize contacts and employees associated with an opportunity
b. Influencer map prioritizes the perceived success of the contacts and colleagues
c. Both a and b
d. None of the above

Answer: c

Explanation:

Influencer Map:

- Influencer map allows you to visualize contacts and employees associated with an opportunity
- It prioritizes the perceived success of these contacts and colleagues
- It helps you close deals by adjusting their position to be larger and closer to the center of the map (to indicate more influence) or smaller and further from the center (to indicate less influence).

16. **Which of the following statement(s) is/are true regarding Opportunity Hierarchy?**

Please choose the correct answer.

a. Opportunity will show all Child Opportunities in hierarchy
b. Parent Opportunity ID cannot be added as a field to the header
c. Both and b
d. None of the above

Answer: a

Explanation:

Opportunity Hierarchy:

- Opportunity Hierarchy can help maintain a hierarchy of parent and child opportunities
- Parent Opportunity ID can be added as a field to the header
- Opportunity will show all Child Opportunities in hierarchy but Parent Hierarchy shows in field

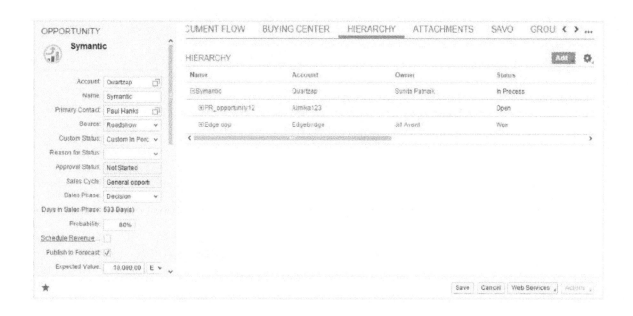

17. **Which of the following statements are true regarding SAP Hybris Cloud for Customer Integration with SAP ERP?**

    Note: There are 2 correct answers to this question.

    a. You have to always create a sales order request or a quote request before creating an order or a quote in ERP
    b. It is possible to directly create a sales order from an opportunity
    c. It is not possible to directly create a quote from an opportunity
    d. By default, an order request or a quote request is created.

    Answer: b, d

    Explanation:

    Until now, you had to always create a sales order request or a quote request before creating an order or a quote in ERP.

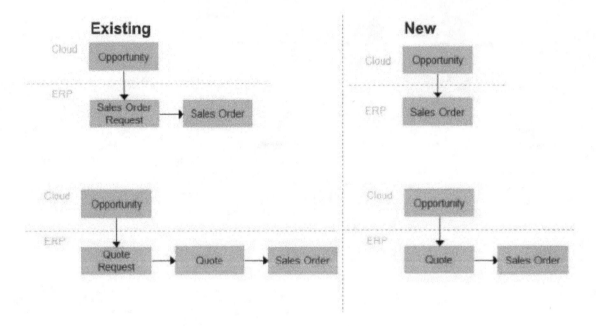

It is now *also* possible to directly create:
- A sales order from an opportunity
- A quote from an opportunity

By default, an order request or a quote request is created.

To use this feature, you need to do the following:
- PO: Adjust PI mapping to decide the document that needs to be created in ERP
- PO: Adjust routing conditions in PI
- HCI: Deploy iFlows

18. **In SAP Hybris Cloud for Customer, Followup Transactions of Sales Quote and Sales Order can be created from which of the following facet of Opportunity?**

Please choose the correct answer.

a. Products
b. Sales Activity
c. Contracts
d. Sales Documents

Answer: d

Explanation:

Follow-Up Transactions in SAP Hybris Cloud for Customer:

Followup Transactions of Sales Quote and Sales Order can be created from Sales Documents facet of Opportunity. All the required information will flow from Opportunity to the target transaction automatically.

19. **Which of the following are the benefits of Opportunity Management?**

   Note: There are 2 correct answers to this question.

   a. Calendar management across multiple channels
   b. Creation of multiple activities at one Shot
   c. Increased revenue by winning more deals
   d. Improved sales forecasting & outcomes

   Answer: c, d

   Explanation:

   Opportunity Management:

   Description:
   - Accurately characterize business opportunities and gain visibility into pipeline health
   - Leverage best practices and collaboration to ensure effective and consistent sales processes

   Key Differentiators:
   - Embedded collaboration and feed

- Flexible sales methodology modeling
- Comprehensive analytics

Benefits:
- Increased revenue by winning more deals
- Improved sales forecasting & outcomes
- Accelerated deals and improved sales effectiveness with pipeline visibility

Calendar management across multiple channels and Creation of multiple activities at one Shot are not the benefits of Opportunity Management.

20. **You can see the SAP ERP pricing information for an Opportunity in which of the following column for each product?**

Please choose the correct answer.

a. Negotiated Price
b. Proposed Price
c. List Price
d. Product Price

Answer: a

Explanation:

SAP ERP Pricing Information for an Opportunity:

- If your solution is integrated with SAP ERP, then you can request SAP ERP pricing information for an opportunity
- You can see the SAP ERP pricing information in the Negotiated Price column for each product.

21. Which of the following attributes are delivered out of the box in Buying Center?

Note: There are 3 correct answers to this question.

a. Attitude
b. Strength of Influence
c. Interaction frequency
d. Name
e. Actions

Answer: a, b, c

Explanation:

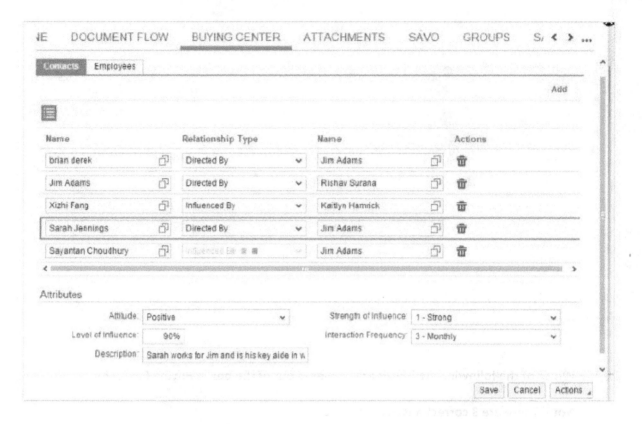

- Relationship attributes set up by relationship types
- Five attributes delivered out of the box
  - Attitude
  - Level of Influence
  - Description
  - Strength of Influence
  - Interaction Frequency

22. **Which of the following report shows the comparison of target revenue, forecast revenue with opportunities in the pipeline?**

Please choose the correct answer.

a. Forecast Opportunity List
b. Forecast Metrics
c. Forecast vs Sales Target vs Pipeline by Month
d. None of the above

Answer: c

Explanation:

Forecast vs Sales Target vs Pipeline by Month shows the comparison of target revenue, forecast revenue with opportunities in the pipeline.

Integration

23. **Which of the following are the ERP technical prerequisites for integrating with SAP Cloud for Customer?**

    Note: There are 3 correct answers to this question.

    a. Minimum ERP 6.0, EHP 0, Support Package 15 (SAP_APPL)
    b. SAP BASIS 6.0, Support Package 15
    c. C4C Add-On CODERINT 600 (COD_ERP_INT 6.00). Requires latest Support Package
    d. Higher EHP for specific functionality
    e. SAP BASIS 5.0, Support Package 15

    Answer: a, c, d

    Explanation:

Integration to SAP ERP does have some technical prerequisites that need to be fulfilled. Before considering an integration project, check with your on premise SAP Basis team to verify the following:

ERP Technical Prerequisites:

- Minimum ERP 6.0, EHP 0, Support Package 15 (SAP_APPL)
- SAP BASIS 7.0, Support Package 18 (SAP_BASIS)
- C4C Add-On CODERINT 600 (COD_ERP_INT 6.00). Requires latest Support Package
- Higher EHP for specific functionality
    - EHP2 for viewing related Sales Order in Accounts
    - EHP3 for viewing related Sales Order in Opportunity
    - EHP5 for viewing related quotes and sales order as PDF in Opportunity

24. **Which of the following is/are the CRM technical prerequisite(s) for integrating with SAP Cloud for Customer?**

Please choose the correct answer.

a. SAP CRM 7.0 EHP 0, Support Package 6 (SAPKU70006)
b. Latest Support Package of BBPCRM
c. C4C Add-On CTMPCD01 700. Requires latest Support Package
d. Only a and b
e. a, b, and c

Answer: e

Explanation:

Integration to SAP CRM does have some technical prerequisites that need to be fulfilled. Before considering an integration project, check with your on premise SAP Basis team to verify the following:

CRM Technical Prerequisites:

- SAP CRM 7.0 EHP 0, Support Package 6 (SAPKU70006)
- Latest Support Package of BBPCRM
- C4C Add-On CTMPCD01 700. Requires latest Support Package

25. **Which of the following is/are common example(s) of why customers require integration of SAP Cloud for Customer with SAP CRM and/or SAP ERP?**

Please choose the correct answer.

a. Get a new division up and running quickly
b. Extend existing SAP CRM platform to new users

c. Looking for a company-wide solution for all Sales, Service, and Marketing organizations (including all subsidiaries and sales offices)
d. Only a and b
e. a, b, and c

Answer: e

Explanation:

The following are some common examples of why customers require integration with SAP CRM and/or SAP ERP.

- Looking for a company-wide solution for all Sales, Service, and Marketing organizations (including all subsidiaries and sales offices)
- Running sales offices or subsidiaries through Cloud solutions with shared master data
- Need SAP CRM on-premise capabilities, however would prefer the SAP Cloud for Customer User Experience (SAP CRM the backbone, SAP Cloud for Customer for the field reps)
- Get a new division up and running quickly
- Extend existing SAP CRM platform to new users
- CRM on-premise is up and running, but want to go "Cloud only" in future, or offer deployment flexibility
- Replacing existing competitor's Cloud SFA solutions with SAP Cloud for Customer and having also SAP CRM OP in
- Start quickly with SFA (or Service) in the Cloud (plus Campaign and Lead Management)

26. **Which of the following is/are the key(s) to successful project management around integration of SAP Cloud for Customer with SAP ERP/SAP CRM applications?**

Please choose the correct answer.

a. Understand that integration requires some configuration
b. Determine early in the project the amount of custom fields
c. Ensure the project team includes functional and integration resources
d. Only a and b
e. a, b, and c

Answer: e

Explanation:

As part of the integration projects, aspects such as network topology, security, firewalls, and reverse proxy will be required so it is critical that your on-premise network and technical team are involved, at least for the connectivity of SAP Cloud for Customer to your on-premise applications.

The following are three keys to successful project management around integration:

- Understand that integration requires some configuration
- Determine early in the project the amount of custom fields
- Ensure the project team includes functional and integration resources

27. **When it's time for quarterly upgrades, which of the following is/are the thing(s) to consider around integration?**

Please choose the correct answer.

a. Existing integrations should continue to work
b. New releases could have new integration flows
c. Testing is highly recommended
d. Only a and b
e. a, b, and c

Answer: e

Explanation:

Upgrade Considerations:

When it's time for quarterly upgrades, things to consider around integration include:

- Existing integrations should continue to work
- New releases could have new integration flows
- Testing is highly recommended
- When using X.509 certificated, ensure they are renewed on schedule

28. **Which of the following statements are true when using MS Outlook with Cloud for Customer?**

Note: There are 2 correct answers to this question.

a. When the service scenario is enabled, e-mails sent from Microsoft Outlook are regarded in SAP Cloud for Customer as activities.
b. Working from MS Outlook, you can create and access contact and account information
c. The SAP Cloud for Customer Add-in for Microsoft Outlook supports scenarios from sales, service, and marketing
d. By synchronizing appointments, tasks or e-mails, you cannot create corresponding activities within SAP Cloud for Customer.

Answer: b, c

Explanation:

The SAP Cloud for Customer Add-in for Microsoft Outlook allows you to synchronize and exchange some information between your e-mail system and SAP Cloud for Customer and supports scenarios from sales, service, and marketing.

Working from MS Outlook, you can create and access contact and account information. You can also view associated items like opportunities and leads.

By synchronizing appointments, tasks or e-mails, you create corresponding activities within SAP Cloud for Customer. You can also add them with reference to an account, campaign, opportunity, or lead.

When the service scenario is enabled, e-mails sent from Microsoft Outlook are not regarded in SAP Cloud for Customer as activities. Instead, they are responses to a ticket.

29. **Before you can begin using MS Outlook and SAP Cloud for Customer, ensure which of the following is complete?**

Note: There are 3 correct answers to this question.

a. Ensure the associated scoping element is selected
b. Enable ActiveX controls in Internet Explorer
c. Add tenant URL to your trusted sites
d. Ensure you have SAP JAM integration
e. Assign required roles and authorizations

Answer: a, b, c

Explanation:

Before you can begin using MS Outlook and SAP Cloud for Customer, ensure the following is complete:

- Ensure the associated scoping element is selected

- Enable ActiveX controls in Internet Explorer

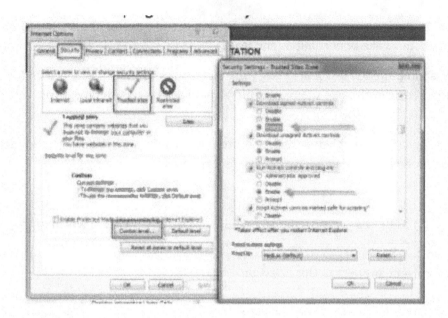

o   Add tenant URL to your trusted sites

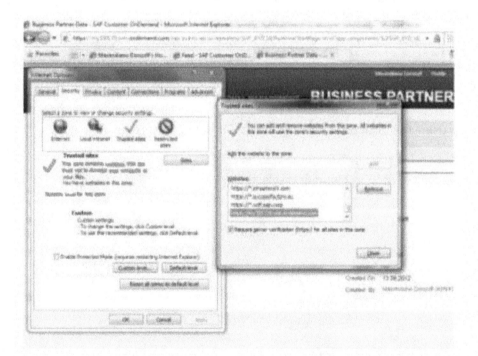

30.   **You can create SAP Jam groups associated with which of the following?**

Note: There are 3 correct answers to this question.

a. Accounts
b. Opportunities
c. Campaigns

d. Tickets

e. Leads

Answer: a, b, d

Explanation:

Integrating SAP Cloud for Customer with SAP Jam provides the built in collaboration tools, groups, and feed that support core business processes.

You can create SAP Jam groups associated with accounts, opportunities, products, and tickets – or generic groups not associated with a specific business object.

31. **The integration setup for SAP Jam involves which of the following?**

Please choose the correct answer.

a. Deciding on user mapping approach

b. Setting up the technical connections

c. Both a and b

d. None of the above

Answer: c

Explanation:

The integration setup for SAP Jam involves:

- Deciding on user mapping approach
- Setting up the technical connections

You also need to make sure you've selected the associated scoping element:

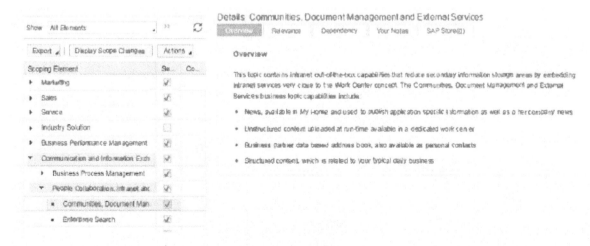

32. **Which of the following are the main configuration activities related to SAP Cloud for Social Engagement?**

Note: There are 2 correct answers to this question.

a. Setting up export runs
b. Setting up channels
c. Adjusting how messages are prioritized
d. Defining work distribution rules to route messages from legacy systems

Answer: b, c

Explanation:

Using SAP Cloud for Social Engagement you can deliver a great customer experience by listening to and engaging with your customers via social media.

Find the most critical messages, and use enterprise data to glean customer insight.

Collaborate within your team or across the organization to resolve issues efficiently and effectively.

The main configuration activities related to SAP Cloud for Social Engagement are:

- Setting up channels
- Setting up import runs
- Adjusting how messages are prioritized
- Defining work distribution rules to route messages from social medial channels

33. **Which of the following are the typical issues encountered around integration?**

Note: There are 2 correct answers to this question.

a. The customer is on the correct service pack (SP) required for the integration
b. General connectivity takes up to 2 weeks because networking resources are not available
c. The customer says they have the On-Premise resource, but that resource is not an expert.
d. The customer has some type of configuration that requires unique integration

Answer: c, d

Explanation:

Typical issues encountered around integration:

- The customer is not on the correct service pack (SP) required for the integration (use the prerequisites to learn early if upgrades to On-Premise applications are required prior to the integration project).

- General connectivity takes up to 4 weeks because networking resources are not available. Before the project starts, enlist the networking personnel. In their view, SAP Cloud for Customer is an internet application that needs access inside of the firewall.
- The customer says they have the On-Premise resource, but that resource is not an expert. Therefore an SAP/Partner resource must supplement this gap. It is critical you have a skilled SAP ERP or SAP CRM technical resource available for the integration.
- The customer has some type of configuration that requires unique integration. For example, employees are set up as org units or business partners instead of employees. Functional On-Premise and cloud experts must be involved to understand functional impact of the integration.

User Management

34. **There are how many access restrictions available in SAP Cloud for Customer?**

    Please choose the correct answer.

    a. 1
    b. 2
    c. 3
    d. 4

    Answer: c

    Explanation:

    Select the view for which you want to restrict access rights and choose the corresponding access restriction:

    - No Access (only available as a restriction for write access)
      The user has no write access
    - Unrestricted
      The user has access to all business data related to the view.
    - Restricted
      The user only has access to specific business data, depending on the access context. If you select restricted, you can restrict read and write access on the basis of predefined restriction rules that you can choose from the Restriction Rule dropdown list.

Product and Pricing

35. **Which of the following are the benefits of Pricing?**

Note: There are 2 correct answers to this question.

a. Consistent pricing across all customer interactions
b. Improved sales coverage through extended market reach
c. Low maintenance cost using standard pricing integration with ERP and CRM
d. Forecast based on multiple dimensions

Answer: a, c

Explanation:

Description:
- Different pricing options: Stand alone, ERP/CRM external pricing or ERP/CRM integrated pricing using predefined integration in order to be consistent across all customer interactions.

Key Differentiators:
- Standard integration for pricing and currency conversion rates with ERP and CRM

Benefits:
- Consistent pricing across all customer interactions
- Low maintenance cost using standard pricing integration with ERP and CRM

Improved sales coverage through extended market reach and Forecast based on multiple dimensions are not the benefits of Pricing.

36.   **Which of the following statement(s) is/are true?**

Please choose the correct answer.

a. Price elements such as freight, or surcharge are not essential for the total value calculation
b. Price master data can be maintained in the work center PRODUCTS
c. SAP Hybris Cloud for Sales contains a predefined set of price elements
d. Only b and c
e. a, b, and c

Answer: d

Explanation:

- As a basic rule pricing depends on the relevant price master data, which derives mainly from a price list which determines a mandatory list price and several optional discount lists, which determines the discounts.
- Other price elements such as freight, or surcharge are essential for the total value calculation.
- Price master data can be maintained in the work center PRODUCTS.

- SAP Hybris Cloud for Sales contains a predefined set of price elements; some of them can be activated in the scoping of the Business Configuration and Fine-tuning.

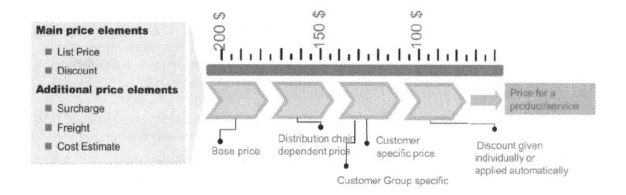

37.   **Which of the following statements are true regarding Internal Pricing in Sales Quotes/Sales Orders?**

Note: There are 2 correct answers to this question.

a. List Price cannot be determined automatically depending on the relevant price list
b. List Price cannot be manually overwritten
c. Additional price elements are not derived from any discount list.
d. Discount (%) can be manually entered or determined through the relevant discount lists

Answer: c, d

Explanation:

Pricing Result
- Pricing can be easily overwritten in the table view of the sales quote.
- Important price information is displayed at a glance.

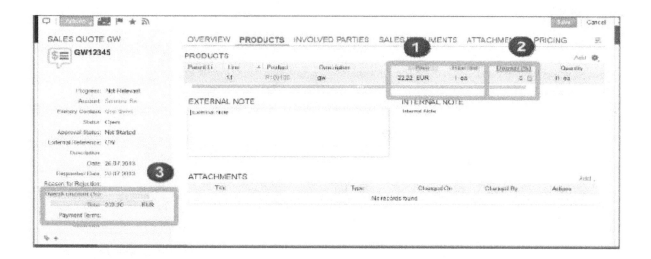

1. List Price: Mandatory price element, which is automatically determined depending on the relevant price list. The List Price can manually be overwritten.

2. Discount (%): Optional price element, which can be manually entered or determined through the relevant discount lists. If the system determines several discounts, these corresponding fields cannot be edited here. In this case, you can view and maintain the discount details in the Pricing tab. Discounts can manually be overwritten.

3. Additional Price Elements: A further Overall Discount (%) applicable to the calculated total item net value can be maintained manually. This is not derived from any discount list.

38. **Which of the following statement(s) is/are true regarding Internal Pricing?**

Please choose the correct answer.

a. SAP Hybris Cloud for Sales offer tax determination with internal pricing.
b. In Total Pricing, you can view and update pricing details for selected line items
c. Both a and b
d. None of the above

Answer: d

Explanation:

Detailed Pricing Result
- Detailed pricing can be viewed and changed in the Pricing tab of the sales quote.
- Additional price elements such as surcharges can be added to the pricing result in the pricing tab.
- Some price elements can be adjusted on item level for selected line items or for the complete document.

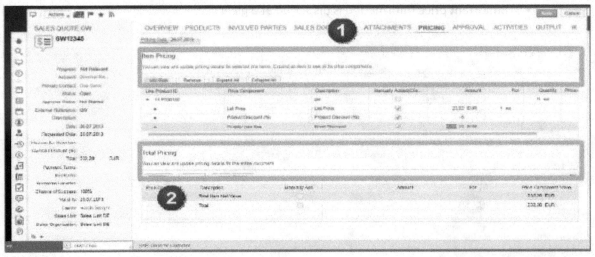

1. Item Pricing: You can view and update pricing details for selected line items. Expand an item to see all its relevant price components. In case input fields are grayed out like tax* the user cannot change the data here. In addition, other price elements such as surcharges can be added to a line item here.

2. Total Pricing: You can view and update pricing details for the entire document. In addition, some other price elements can be added here, such as Overall Discount (%).

*Note: SAP Hybris Cloud for Sales does not offer tax determination with internal pricing.

39. **Which of the following is/are the key feature(s) for Price Master Data?**

Please choose the correct answer.

a. Price Elements
b. Price Master Maintenance
c. Quantity and Currency Conversion
d. Only a and b
e. a, b, and c

Answer: e

Explanation:

Key Features for Internal Pricing:

The following Key Features are available:

- **Price Elements**
  - List Price, Product Discount (%)
  - Additional Price Elements

- **Price Master Maintenance**
  - Price Mass Change
  - Price Scales

- **Quantity and Currency Conversion**

40. **Which of the following statements are true?**

Note: There are 2 correct answers to this question.

a. SAP Hybris Cloud for Sales supports discounts in percentage and fixed discount lists.
b. Discount Lists do not have a validity period
c. To determine the product discounts for a product or service, the system checks ALL discount lists that fit the parameters passed from the sales document

d. The discount lists are maintained as price master data in the DISCOUNT LIST View.

Answer: c, d

Explanation:

Main Price Element: Product Discount (%)

Product Discount (%)
- Product Discounts are centrally defined and managed in Discount Lists.
- The system takes multiple parameters into account in order to enable flexible pricing.

- Discount Lists: The following discount lists are available in the system: Customer Specific Discount Products, Overall Customer Discount, Overall Customer Group Discount, Customer Specific Discount List by Product Category.
- Discount List Overview: The discount lists are maintained as price master data in the DISCOUNT LIST View. They have a validity period, need to be released before they are active and can require approval.
- Discount Determination: To determine the product discounts for a product or service, the system checks ALL discount lists that fit the parameters passed from the sales document such as customer, customer group, product, product category and pricing date.

Determination of Discount Lists
- The system checks for all Discount Lists.
- Different from the calculation of the List Price, all relevant Product Discounts will be considered in the price calculation.
- SAP Hybris Cloud for Sales supports discounts in percentage, no fixed discount lists.

- (Discounted are always the discounted values, e.g. List Price =100 USD, 1st discount 10% = 10 USD, 2nd discount 10% = 9 USD, 3rd discount 10% = 8, 10 USD)

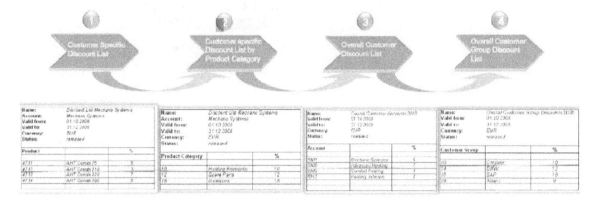

41.   **Which of the following are the Main price elements?**

Note: There are 2 correct answers to this question.

a. Surcharge
b. Discount
c. List Price
d. Freight

Answer: b, c

Explanation:

- As a basic rule pricing depends on the relevant price master data, which derives mainly from a price list which determines a mandatory list price and several optional discount lists, which determines the discounts.
- Other price elements such as freight, or surcharge are essential for the total value calculation.
- Price master data can be maintained in the work center PRODUCTS.
- SAP Hybris Cloud for Sales contains a predefined set of price elements; some of them can be activated in the scoping of the Business Configuration and Fine-tuning.

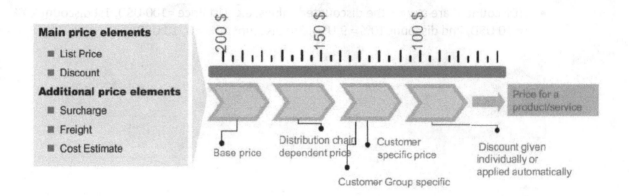

Main price elements
- List Price
- Discount

Additional price elements
- Surcharge
- Freight
- Cost Estimate

Base price

Distribution chain dependent price

Customer specific price

Customer Group specific

Price for a product/service

Discount given individually or applied automatically

42. **Which of the following view allows you to create, maintain and mass update price master data?**

Please choose the correct answer.

a. PRICE LIST
b. DISCOUNT LIST
c. PRODUCT LISTS
d. PRODUCT CATEGORIES

Answer: a

Explanation:

Pricing View:
- View PRICE LIST in part of the Work Center (WoC) PRODUCTS
- This view allows you to create, maintain and mass update price master data such as price lists, discount lists

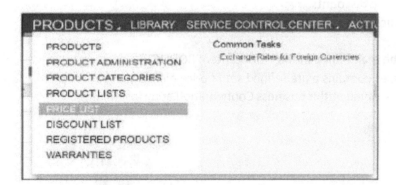

Main Views:
- Price Lists: Price lists of different types (base price, distribution chain specific and customer specific) can be maintained

- Discount Lists: Discounts lists can be maintained in different granularities (overall customer group, overall customer, customer product specific and customer product category specific)

▼ General Business Data

   ▶ Business Partners

   ▶ Employees and Service Agents

   ▶ Products

   ▼ Product and Service Pricing

      ■ Sales Price and Discount Lists

      ■ Sales Price Specifications

      ■ Communication for Product and Service Pricing

43.   **Which of the following price lists are available in the system?**

Note: There are 3 correct answers to this question.

a. Customer Specific
b. Distribution Chain Specific
c. Base Price Lists
d. Overall Customer Discount
e. Customer Specific Discount List by Product Category

Answer: a, b, c

Explanation:

List Price
- List prices are centrally defined and managed in Price Lists.
- The system takes multiple parameters into account in order to enable flexible pricing.

Price Lists: The following price lists are available in the system: Customer Specific, Distribution Chain* Specific and Base Price Lists**.

Price List Overview: The price lists are maintained as price master data in the Pricing View. They have a validity period, need to be released before they are active and optionally can require approval.

Price List Determination: To determine the net list price of a product or service, the system checks all price lists that fit the parameters passed from the sales document such as customer, sales organization, product, product category, and posting date.

* A Distribution Chain represent the combination of a Sales Organization and a Distribution Channel.

** Only one Base Price List can be released.

44.   **Which of the following statement(s) is/are true regarding Price Scales?**

Please choose the correct answer.

a. You cannot define from-scales for prices which depend on different quantities.
b. The scale you maintained as master data determines how values are calculated.
c. Both and b
d. None of the above

Answer: b

Explanation:

Price Scales:
* You can define from-scales for prices which depend on different quantities.
* The scale you maintained as master data determines how values are calculated. For example, you can use a scale to define that a single boiler costs $788 but if you buy at least 10 boilers the price decreases to $750 per unit.
* NOTE: Use a "from" price to define the price range and start with a value 1 each.

45.   **Which of the following statements are true regarding Price Calculation?**

Note: There are 2 correct answers to this question.

a. The document currency is defaulted from the account master sales data

b. A prerequisite for Quantity Conversion is that the quantity conversions are maintained in the product master data

c. In SAP Hybris Cloud for Sales the system doesn't automatically calculate currency and quantity conversions that lead to the determination of the total value for the sales quote.

d. Exchange Rates update cannot be triggered through SAP ERP Integration

Answer: a, b

Explanation:

Price Calculation:

- In SAP Hybris Cloud for Sales the system automatically calculates currency and quantity conversions that lead to the determination of the total value for the sales quote.
- Currency and Quantity conversions depend on further master data maintenance.

Currency Conversion
- During the price calculation, currency conversion occurs if the currency of the price master data differs from the document currency, depending on the exchange rates maintained as master data (common task in Products view)
- The document currency is defaulted from the account master sales data

Quantity Conversion
- During the price calculation, quantity conversion occurs if the unit of measure requested in the document differs from the price unit maintained in the price list
- A prerequisite is that the quantity conversions are maintained in the product master data

Exchange Rates update can be triggered through SAP ERP Integration.

46. **Which of the following statement(s) is/are true regarding Offline Pricing?**

Please choose the correct answer.

a. Scales information is currently used in offline price calculation

b. New work center view "Prices" under Products work center is used to view prices stored in price specification business object in SAP Hybris Cloud for Customer. These price specifications are currently used for internal pricing.

c. Both a and b

d. None of the above

Answer: d

Explanation:

Offline Pricing - Transfer ERP Prices to SAP Hybris Cloud for Customer:

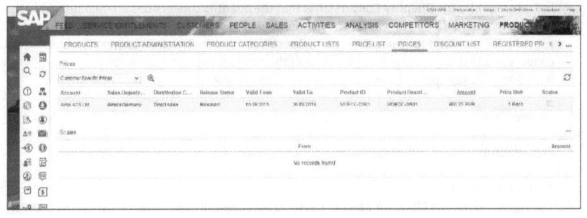

- New work center view "Prices" under Products work center to view prices stored in price specification business object in SAP Hybris Cloud for Customer. Note, these price specifications are currently not used for internal pricing.
- Sales Area specific Base Price and Customer Specific Price supported with date validity and quantity based scales. Note, scales information is currently not used in offline price calculation and is planned in roadmap.
- Standard integration service provided for transfer of prices from SAP ECC (replicate sales area and sales area specific customer price conditions) into SAP Hybris Cloud for Customer.

47.   **Which of the following statement(s) is/are true?**

Please choose the correct answer.

a. Offline pricing will be supported in context of external pricing setup
b. New field "Estimated Price" available offline only on Order Item Proposal (Fast Order Entry) with Manual Discounts fields - % and absolute
c. Both a and b
d. None of the above

Answer: b

Explanation:

Usage of Offline Pricing in Offline Order Entry:
- New field "Estimated Price" available offline only on Order Item Proposal (Fast Order Entry) with Manual Discounts fields - % and absolute (mapped to PPE1 and PPE2). Supported in extended SAP Hybris Cloud for Customer App Cloud4CustEx mobile app only.
- Fixed value calculation: Estimated Price = [{(Customer Specific Price or Base Price) x Quantity} - Discount (%) - Absolute Discount]
- During sync, manual discounts are transferred to SAP Hybris Cloud for Customer to PPE1 and PPE2 and to ECC on order simulate or/and transfer. Note, that offline pricing will be supported in context of external pricing setup.

48.   **Which of the following is NOT an Activity type?**

Please choose the correct answer.

a. Appointment
b. E-mail
c. Contract
d. Phone call

Answer: c

Explanation:

Activity Management - Key Features:

Activity Types:
- Appointments
- Tasks
- Phone calls
- E-Mails

General Activity Features:

- Notes or message area for participants
- Attachments
- Status (open, in process, complete)
- Work set list view
- Quick view
- Reference an account and contact
- Reference a lead or opportunity

49. **Which of the following statement(s) is/are true regarding Activity Management – Calendar View?**

Please choose the correct answer.

a. Create appointments via iPad by tapping
b. Work with a color-coded global calendar
c. View appointments, visits, and phone calls for a user in the calendar view
d. Only a and b
e. a, b, and c

Answer: e

Explanation:

Activity Management-Calendar View:

- View appointments, visits, and phone calls for a user in the calendar view
- Create appointments via iPad by tapping
- Check multiple views - day, week, month, and list (additional work week view on browser)
- View other user's calendar on browser if authorized
- Work with a color-coded global calendar

50. **Which of the following statement(s) is/are true regarding Activity Management – Emails?**

Please choose the correct answer.

a. Synchronize with Microsoft Outlook 2007 or 2010 or 2013
b. Transfer inbound or outbound e-mails from MS Outlook to SAP Hybris Cloud for Customer
c. Reference other SAP Hybris Cloud for Customer items while in Outlook and find the e-mail listed with those objects
d. Only a and b
e. a, b, and c

Answer: e

Explanation:

Activity Management – Emails:

- View familiar e-mail details common to other systems
- Access attachments synched from MS Outlook
- Review e-mail message
- View To and Cc recipients
- Reference other SAP Hybris Cloud for Customer items while in Outlook and find the e-mail listed with those objects (accounts, leads, opportunities, or campaigns)
- Create e-mails in your local e-mail client
    - Add e-mails back to Cloud for Sales only through Outlook 2007 or 2010 or 2013 (E-mail details cannot be edited once synchronized to SAP Hybris Cloud for Sales)
- Synchronize with Microsoft Outlook 2007 or 2010 or 2013
- Transfer inbound or outbound e-mails from MS Outlook to SAP Hybris Cloud for Customer
- Associate to an account and lead, opportunity, or campaign

51.   Which of the following is/are the feature(s) of Partner Channel Management?

Please choose the correct answer.

a. Industry capabilities
b. Collaborative opportunity management

c. Partner lead scoring and routing
d. Only a and c
e. a, b, and c

Answer: e

Explanation:

Key Features:
- Effective Partner data management, provisioning and access rights
- Partner lead scoring and routing
- Collaborative opportunity management
- Industry capabilities

Benefits:
- Incremental revenue growth
- Improved value prop through partner value add
- Improved sales coverage including access to inaccessible accounts

52.   **Which of the following statement(s) is/are true regarding Deal Registration?**

Please choose the correct answer.

a. Status of the deal can be viewed as accepted/Rejected or converted
b. In case a deal is converted to an opportunity, the partner can view the opportunity ID and then work on the assigned opportunity
c. Deals can be created on the partner portal
d. Only a and c
e. a, b, and c

Answer: e

Explanation:

Manage Deal Registration:

- Create deals on the partner portal
- Display overview
- Filter (all, my, converted leads)
- Sort order (by name, level, status)
- View status of the deal as accepted/Rejected or converted
- In case a deal is converted to an opportunity, the partner can view the opportunity ID and then work on the assigned opportunity

53. **Which of the following is NOT involved in PCM Registration flow?**

Please choose the correct answer.

a. User
b. SAP IDS/Other IDS
c. SAP Hybris Cloud for Customer Backend
d. Cloud Portal
e. SAP BW

Answer: e

Explanation:

PCM Registration Flow - High Level System Landscape:

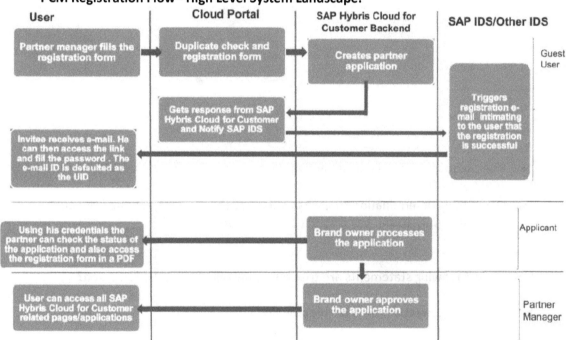

Quotation and Sales Order Management

54. **In Quotation Management, Free Goods Determination supports which of the following determination(s)?**

Please choose the correct answer.

a. Inclusive
b. Exclusive
c. Both a and b
d. None of the above

Answer: c

Explanation:

Free Goods Determination:

- The "Request External Pricing" action returns free goods from the On Premise system (CRM or ERP)
- Free Goods Determination supports EXCLUSIVE (buy ten and get one free) and INCLUSIVE (buy 10 and pay only 9) determinations

55. **Which of the following statements are true regarding Bill of Material Explosion?**

Note: There are 2 correct answers to this question.

a. If a Bill of Material is relevant to a quoted product, the BOM items will be shown in the Sales Quote
b. The action "Request External Pricing" triggers the import and explosion of the Bill of Material from SAP ERP or CRM
c. Only Multi-level Bill of Material supported
d. Pricing is not editable on the header item

Answer: a, b

Explanation:

Bill of Material Explosion:

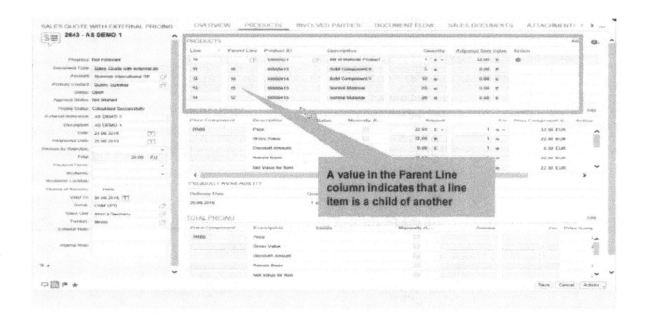

A value in the Parent Line column indicates that a line item is a child of another

- If a Bill of Material is relevant to a quoted product, the BOM items will be shown in the Sales Quote
- The action "Request External Pricing" triggers the import and explosion of the Bill of Material from SAP ERP or CRM
- Pricing and quantity are editable only on the header item
- Single level and Multi-level Bill of Material supported

56. **Which of the following are the benefits of Quotation Management?**

Note: There are 2 correct answers to this question.

a. Calendar management across multiple channels
b. Creation of multiple activities at one Shot
c. Accelerate sales cycles
d. Improve revenue and margin

Answer: c, d

Explanation:

Quotation Management:

Description:
- Flexible quoting capabilities enable you to deliver compelling offers, provide consistent accurate pricing, and streamline the sales process

Key Differentiators:
- Flexible pricing leveraging native pricing or SAP CRM or ERP Pricing

- Follow-on order creation in ERP

Benefits:
- Accelerate sales cycles
- Improve revenue and margin
- Streamline quote-to-cash and reduce processing errors

Calendar management across multiple channels and Creation of multiple activities at one Shot are not the benefits of Quotation Management.

57. **Which of the following are the features of Quotation Management?**

Note: There are 3 correct answers to this question.

a. Rule based party determination
b. Standard analytical content
c. Change history
d. API support for exporting order documents
e. Order creation in SAP ERP, PDF order capability

Answer: b, c, e

Explanation:

Quotation Management-Features:
- Quotation capabilities such as create, view, update, delete, validity period
- Opportunity management integration
- Pricing and Price Check (native SAP Hybris Cloud for Customer Pricing)
- Basic pricing including list prices, discounts, surcharges (fixed and percentage based)
- Customer specific product lists
- Pricing integration with ERP/CRM (live call via order simulation)
- Campaign integration
- Support of configurable products (through integration)
- Involved party determination
- Notes and attachments
- Rule-based multi-step order approval workflow
- Flexible notifications
- Output management, format templates, language selection in order
- Mobile iPad support including digital signature capture
- Follow-on documents such as activities
- Order replication to SAP ERP, PDF order capability
- SAP Jam integration
- Change history
- API support for importing order documents
- Standard analytical content

58. **Which of the following are the benefits of Order Management?**

Note: There are 2 correct answers to this question.

a. Accelerated sales cycles
b. Improved revenue and margin
c. Forecast based on multiple dimensions
d. Improved value proposition through partner value add

Answer: a, b

Explanation:

Order Management:

Description:
- Flexible order capabilities enable you to deliver fast order entry, provide consistent accurate pricing, and streamline the sales process

Key Differentiators:
- Flexible pricing leveraging native pricing or SAP CRM or ERP Pricing
- Replication of order to ERP

Benefits:
- Accelerated sales cycles
- Streamlined quote-to-cash and reduced processing errors
- Improved revenue and margin

Forecast based on multiple dimensions and improved value proposition through partner value add are not the benefits of Order Management.

59. **Which of the following are the features of Order Management?**

Note: There are 3 correct answers to this question.

a. Rule based party determination
b. Pricing integration with ERP
c. SAP Jam integration
d. Mobile iPad support including digital signature capture
e. API support for exporting order documents

Answer: b, c, d

Explanation:

Order Management-Features:

- Order capabilities such as create, view, update, delete, validity period
- Opportunity and Quotation management integration
- Pricing and Price Check (native SAP Hybris Cloud for Customer Pricing)
- Basic pricing including list prices, discounts, surcharges (fixed and percentage based)
- Customer specific product lists
- Pricing integration with ERP/CRM (live call via order simulation)
- Support of configurable products (through integration)
- Involved party determination
- Notes and attachments
- Rule-based multi-step order approval workflow
- Flexible notifications
- Output management, format templates, language selection in order
- Mobile iPad support including digital signature capture
- Follow-on documents such as activities
- Order replication to SAP ERP, PDF order capability
- SAP Jam integration
- Change history
- API support for importing order documents
- Standard analytical content

60. **Creation of Sales Order can be which of the following?**

Note: There are 2 correct answers to this question.

a. Follow-up of Sales Quote
b. Follow-up of Opportunity
c. Follow-up of Contract
d. Follow-up of Activity

Answer: a, b

Explanation:

Creation of Sales Order can be the following:
- Follow-up of Sales Quote
- Follow-up of Opportunity
- From Account Master Data via Sales Document facet
- Directly from the Sales work center using Sales Quote view
- Copying an existing sales order

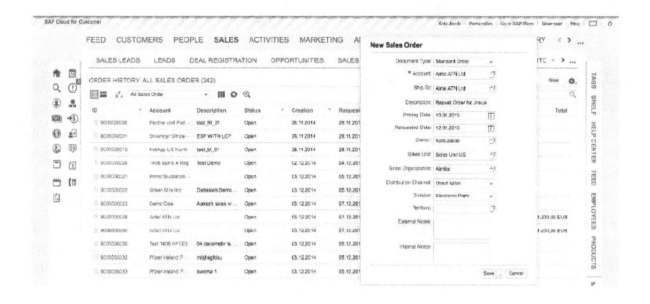

61.   **Which of the following doesn't have a Sales Order Facet?**

Please choose the correct answer.

a. Account
b. Quote
c. Activity
d. Visit

Answer: c

Explanation:

Sales Order Facets in - Account, Quote, & Visit:

- Accounts: Order Facet in Account displaying all orders for this account.
- Visit: Order facet displaying all orders associated to the visit
- Quote: Order facet displaying orders created from that quotation

62.   **In Order Edit of SAP Hybris Cloud for Customer, which of the following are editable fields in header?**

Note: There are 3 correct answers to this question.

a. Quantity
b. Reason for Rejection
c. PO Number
d. Manual Discount
e. UoM

Answer: b, c, d

Explanation:

Orders Edit:
- Orders created in SAP Hybris Cloud for Customer and transferred to ERP can be edited and copied, as well as order downloaded from ERP
- Adding new products
- Changing quantity of non-delivered products
- Changing price/price components of products only if billing is not in process or finished

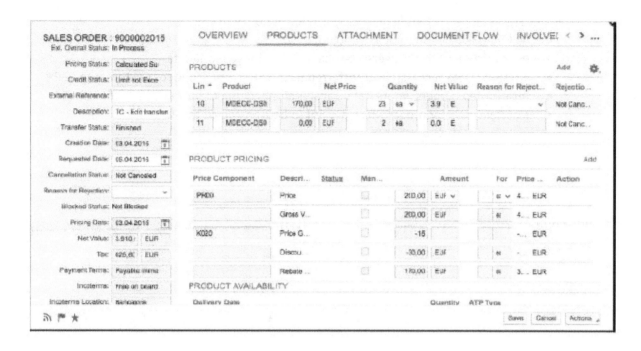

Editable Fields Header:
- Order Description
- Order Reason
- PO Number
- Requested Delivery date
- Currency
- Reason for rejection
- Add Price components
- Manual Discount
- External / Internal Notes

63. **Which of the following are Order Transfer Statuses?**

    Note: There are 3 correct answers to this question.

    a. Not Started
    b. Interrupted
    c. Relevant
    d. Aborted
    e. Finished

    Answer: a, b, e

    Explanation:

    Order Transfer Status Management:

Transfer Status helps to identify objects sync information with ERP
- **Not Started:** Transfer not yet triggered
- **In Process:** Transfer Triggered but handshake not yet complete
- **Finished:** Data successfully transferred from SAP Hybris Cloud for Customer to ERP
- **Interrupted:** Orders where data transfer stopped due to business or Technical error
- **Not Relevant:** for orders which are not to be transferred to ERP

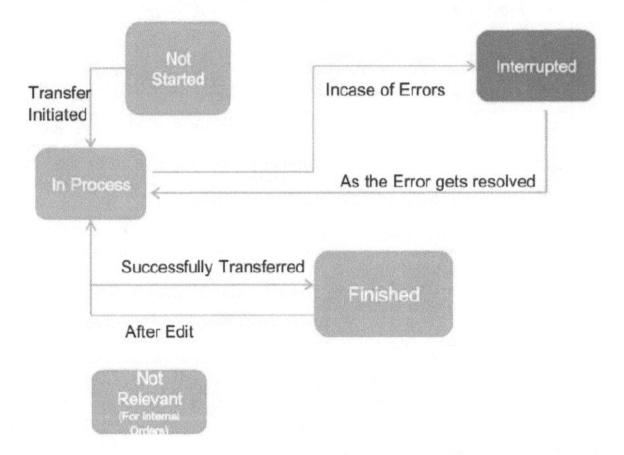

External ID and External System would be updated with corresponding ERP Order number for documents which were successfully transferred to ERP from SAP Hybris Cloud for Customer.

64. **In Order Edit of SAP Hybris Cloud for Customer, which of the following is NOT an editable field in Item?**

Please choose the correct answer.

a. Currency
b. External/Internal Notes
c. Reason for Rejection
d. Requested Delivery Date

Answer: d

Explanation:

Orders Edit:
- Orders created in SAP Hybris Cloud for Customer and transferred to ERP can be edited and copied, as well as order downloaded from ERP
- Adding new products
- Changing quantity of non-delivered products
- Changing price/price components of products only if billing is not in process or finished

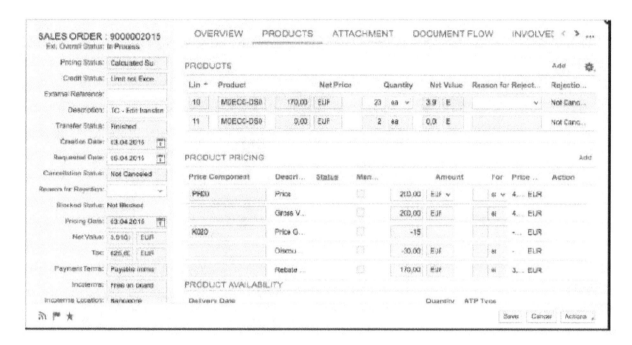

Editable Fields Item:
- Quantity
- Currency
- UoM
- External / Internal Notes
- Reason for Rejection
- Add Price components

65. **Which of the following action returns ATP result from On Premise system (CRM or ERP)?**

Please choose the correct answer.

a. Request External Pricing
b. Request ATP
c. Return External Pricing
d. Return ATP

Answer: a

Explanation:

Product Availability Check:

The action "Request External Pricing" returns ATP result from On Premise system (CRM or ERP).

Personalization and Extensibility

66.   **Which of the following enables individual users to modify their own view of screens?**

       Please choose the correct answer.

       a. Personalization
       b. Adaptation
       c. Both a and b
       d. None of the above

       Answer: a

       Explanation:

SAP Cloud for Customer provides several features that enable you to customize fields, screen layouts, and output forms.

Personalization enables individual users to modify their own view of screens. It impacts only the user making the change to a screen. This allows users to tailor the system to the way that they use it on a daily (or regular) basis.

Administrators can disable this feature via Adapt > Company Settings > Disable User Personalization Features.

Adaptation refers to a set of tools administrators can use to add or modify fields, change master screen layouts, assign screen layouts to specific roles, restrict dropdown list values, and modify output forms. You can also migrate adaptation changes from one system to another.

67.   **Which of the following refers to a set of tools administrators can use to add or modify fields, change master screen layouts, assign screen layouts to specific roles, restrict dropdown list values, and modify output forms?**

Please choose the correct answer.

a. Personalization
b. Adaptation
c. Both a and b
d. None of the above

Answer: b

Explanation:

Personalization enables individual users to modify their own view of screens. It impacts only the user making the change to a screen. This allows users to tailor the system to the way that they use it on a daily (or regular) basis.

Administrators can disable this feature via Adapt > Company Settings > Disable User Personalization Features

Adaptation refers to a set of tools administrators can use to add or modify fields, change master screen layouts, assign screen layouts to specific roles, restrict dropdown list values, and modify output forms. You can also migrate adaptation changes from one system to another.

68. **You can define which of the following properties for an extension field?**

   Note: There are 3 correct answers to this question.

   a. Mandatory
   b. Read only
   c. Visible
   d. Write only
   e. Optional

   Answer: a, b, c

   Explanation:

   Once you've created an extension field, you can define further field properties such as whether the field should be mandatory or read only.

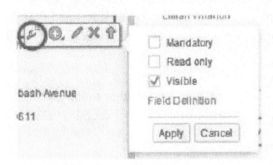

69. **Which of the following template(s) can be customized to meet your specific business needs?**

   Please choose the correct answer.

   a. Form templates
   b. Master templates
   c. Both a and b
   d. None of the above

   Answer: c

   Explanation:

   Both form and master templates can be customized to meet your specific business needs.

ADMINISTRATOR ‚ CUSTOMER SERVICE ‚ TICKETS DATA PRIVACY MAN/

GENERAL SETTINGS

USERS

 EMPLOYEES

 BUSINESS USERS

SERVICE AND SOCIAL SETTINGS

SALES AND MARKETING SETTINGS

BUSINESS FLEXIBILITY

MASHUP WEB SERVICES

MASHUP AUTHORING

MASTER TEMPLATE MAINTENANCE

FORM TEMPLATE MAINTENANCE

MICROSOFT OFFICE® TEMPLATE MAINT.

FLEXIBILITY CHANGE LOG

70.   **There are how many ways to customize forms?**

        Please choose the correct answer.

        a. 2
        b. 3
        c. 4
        d. 5

        Answer: a

        Explanation:

        There are 2 ways to customize forms:

        - Using the easy form editor
        - Using the Adobe LiveCycle Designer

        For more complex editing, some experience with the LiveCycle Designer is recommended.

        It is important that these custom forms be identified early in the project to allow enough time for development and avoid any project delays. If the requirement comes late in the project, it will likely cause project delays. It is also important to understand and communicate the associated cost for this development.

Before development begins it is important that detailed requirements are gathered that can be passed to the development team.

Data Migration

71.   **Which of the following is/are risk(s) resulting due to incorrect/improper Data Migration?**

Please choose the correct answer.

a. Decreased end user productivity due to bad data and incorrect information
b. Mishandling of open transactions impacting operations
c. Both a and b
d. None of the above

Answer: c

Explanation:

Data Migration is a critical path item for every project. Without successfully transferring data from legacy applications to SAP Cloud for Customer, you expose the project and the customer to unnecessary risks such as:

- Decreased end user productivity due to bad data and incorrect information
- Mishandling of open transactions impacting operations

72.   **Data Migration process incorporates which of the following steps?**

Note: There are 3 correct answers to this question.

a. Cleanse
b. Extract Source Data
c. Populate Migration Templates
d. Security model
e. Transport the models

Answer: a, b, c

Explanation:

This process incorporates the following primary steps:

1.	Schedule	Create a precise project plan for all tasks regarding migration.
2.	Cleanse	Cleanse the legacy data that will be migrated to the SAP Cloud for Customer solution to avoid technical errors during migration and usability problems.
3.	Extract Source Data	Extraction of source data from the legacy system can be automated or done manually. It is the responsibility of the customer.
4.	Populate Migration Templates	Create the source files by entering the cleansed and extracted legacy data in the migration templates predefined by SAP. The templates provide a framework to structure source data closely to SAP Cloud for Customer structure.
5.	Test Migration	Perform test imports of the source data. A successful test migration ensures a safe, final cutover migration.
6.	Verify	Verify the source data by using it in the test scenarios.
7.	Cutover Migration	Perform the final import of source data to the production system using the migration tool.

73. Which of the following are NOT the drivers for selecting a manual migration approach?

Note: There are 3 correct answers to this question.

a. High data volumes
b. Lack of legacy data
c. Integration is in scope
d. Requirement for performing multiple loads in different systems
e. Legacy data is too unstructured

Answer: a, c, d

Explanation:

Data Migration Methods (no integration to ECC or CRM)

Manual Migration	Tool-Supported Migration
Is executed by your project team members the regular transactions in the SAP Cloud for Customer solution.	Is executed by your project team leveraging the provided **MS Excel templates** and the SAP Cloud for Customer migration tool.
Drivers for selecting a manual migration approach: ▪ Low data volumes ▪ Lack of legacy data ▪ Legacy data is too unstructured ▪ Migration template for a specific object is not available	Drivers for selecting a template based approach: ▪ High data volumes ▪ Available time period to load the data in the Production system For example, if all data needs to be loaded over a weekend manual migration is not possible in most cases ▪ Requirement for performing multiple data loads in different systems You can fill the template once and load it multiple times, for example, for test loads in the DM Test system and final load in the Production system ▪ Preferred method in case integration is in scope

74. **Which of the following statements are true about Data Migration Templates?**

    Note: There are 2 correct answers to this question.

    a. The template structure is predefined, but can be changed
    b. Each template contains just one tab that has all the data grouped into it
    c. Each template provides field definitions, which are used during the population of the templates
    d. A template is available for each migration object that supports tool-supported migration

    Answer: c, d

    Explanation:

    The Data Migration templates are provided by SAP and are used to migrate data into SAP Cloud for Customer. They provide a structure and framework for the data that must be migrated from the customer's legacy system(s).

    - The template structure is predefined and cannot be changed (extended or modified) and any changes made to the template structure will result in upload errors.
    - A template is available for each migration object that supports tool-supported migration
    - Each template contains different tabs that group the data into logical units
    - Each template provides field definitions, which are used during the population of the templates

75. **It is important that testing is not seen as which of the following?**

Please choose the correct answer.

a. End user training
b. Time for business process optimization
c. Both a and b
d. None of the above

Answer: c

Explanation:

Testing ensures that the business processes can be successfully executed in SAP Cloud for Customer and minimizes significant problems during and after Go-Live.

It is important that testing is not seen as the following:

- End user training (or key user training)
  The hands-on experience during the testing phase will significantly increase the understanding and confidence level of testers, but should not be considered training
- Time for business process optimization (that is, this is not the time to implement improvements to the business processes).

The test plan is used to define the test scope and ensure that all business scenarios and variants are covered by the test scenarios as well as the planning and tracking of test scenario execution.

76. **Which of the following is/are example(s) of a plug-in for the Readiness Acceptance Q-Gate?**

Please choose the correct answer.

a. When a customer purchases data migration services for SAP to perform the data imports
b. When a partner builds a custom solution extension for SAP Cloud for Customer
c. Both a and b
d. None of the above

Answer: c

Explanation:

The Solution Testing stream begins with the customer preparing all testing documentation. Then the customer fully tests all end-to-end scenarios using migrated data. This should include analytics, forms, user access, integration, custom solution extensions etc.

The project team begins to prepare for the cutover by identifying and scheduling the necessary tasks and resources.

An example of a plug-in for the Readiness Acceptance Q-Gate is when a customer purchases data migration services for SAP to perform the data imports. Another example is when a partner builds a custom solution extension for SAP Cloud for Customer.

Here again, an agile approach allows for several iterations of data migration, integration setup and solution testing prior to executing the Readiness Acceptance Q-Gate. All testing issues must be resolved or an alternative solution identified before completing the Q-Gate.

Sales Planning and Forecasting

77. **How many version(s) can be active at a given point of time?**

Please choose the correct answer.

a. 1
b. 2
c. 3
d. 4

Answer: a

Explanation:

Maintain Versions:

- Maintain different versions of Sales Target Plan
- For example, create an optimistic version and a pessimistic version
- Only one version can be active at a given point of time

78. **Sales manager can plan sales target based on which of the following?**

Please choose the correct answer.

a. Value

b. Volume

c. Both a and b

d. None of the above

Answer: c

Explanation:

- Update values and press upload to update the value in backend system
- Sales manager can plan based on value or volume
- Plan sales target based on different dimensions selected while defining plan structure

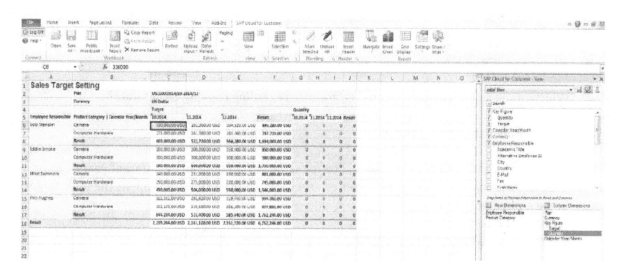

79.   **Which of the following are the key attributes of Sales Forecasting?**

Note: There are 3 correct answers to this question.

a. Analytical Integration

b. Business User Centricity

c. Multi-level Overrides

d. Unidimensional Forecasting

e. Multi language capability

Answer: a, b, c

Explanation:

Below given are the key value drivers of Sales Forecasting:

Key Attributes		
Multi-dimensional Forecasting	>	Forecast based on Opportunity, account, employee, sales organization, territory, product, product category, forecast category
Analytical Integration	>	Uses the reporting interface in MS Excel to maintain and analyze forecasts. Pre-defined specialized dashboard to provide more insights into the forecasts
Multi-level Overrides	>	Allows each user to maintain overrides in their own forecasts at every level of the organizational hierarchy
Business User Centricity	>	Ease of use with a very simple interface to create and update forecasts

80. **Which of the following statement(s) is/are true regarding copying target data?**

Please choose the correct answer.

a. The source and target horizon should be for same period but can be different years
b. Before making a copy, Sales Manager can preview the performance vis-a-vis the sales target in the embedded chart.
c. Both a and b
d. None of the above

Answer: c

Explanation:

Copy Target Data:

- Copy Target data from an existing plan
- This will provide a baseline for planning - for example, copy last year's target and increase it by 10% for this year's target
- Before making a copy, Sales Manager can preview the performance vis-a-vis the sales target in the embedded chart.

The source and target horizon should be for same period but can be different years

New Sales Target Plan

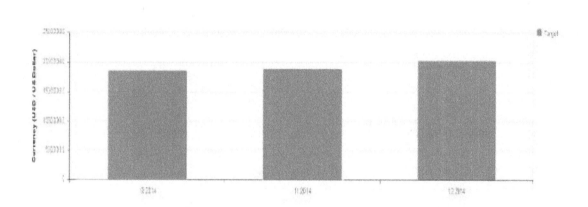

81.   Sales manager can use which of the following report to monitor their direct reportee's progress vis-a-vis the sales targets?

Please choose the correct answer.

a. Sales Target/Pipeline by Employee
b. Sales Forecast by Employee
c. Sales Target/Pipeline by Reportee
d. Sales Forecast by Reportee

Answer: a

Explanation:

Analytics:

- Sales manager can use 'Sales Target/Pipeline by Employee' report to monitor their direct reportee's progress vis-a-vis the sales targets
- Sales manager can toggle the report view between 'By Employees', 'By Month', etc.
- Employees can review their performance using 'My Progress: Sales Target/Pipeline for Employees' report

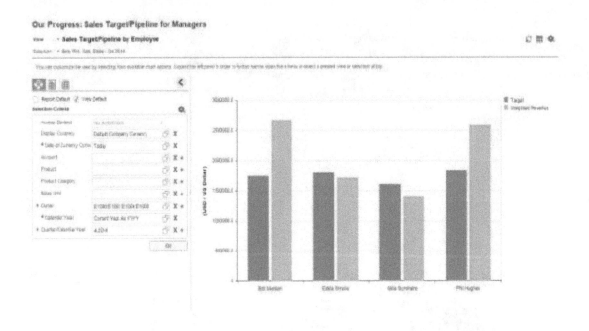

82. **Which of the following statements are true about Forecast Inspector?**

Note: There are 2 correct answers to this question.

a. Even for a forecast in submitted status, new versions can be submitted at any point in time
b. Managers cannot send forecast back for revision
c. Only inactive version can be edited
d. User can have more than one inactive version at a given point in time

Answer: a, c

Explanation:

Forecast Inspector:
Managers can send forecast back for revision. User can have only one inactive version at a given point in time.

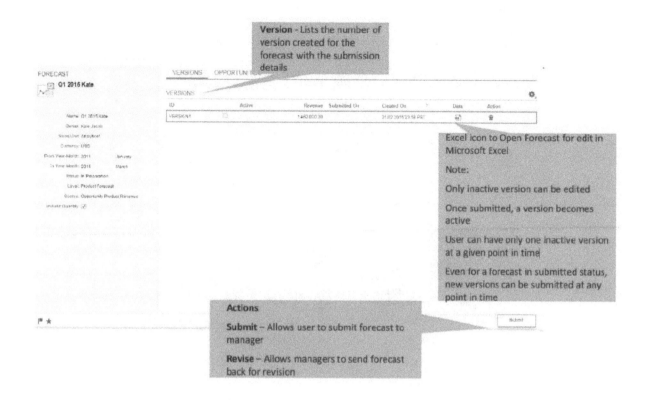

83. **Which of the following statement(s) is/are true regarding maintaining forecast?**

Please choose the correct answer.

a. The forecast revenue is distributed and stored at the lowest level
b. User can save and modify user specific views
c. Both a and b
d. None of the above

Answer: c

Explanation:

The forecast revenue is distributed and stored at the lowest level. User can save and modify user specific views.

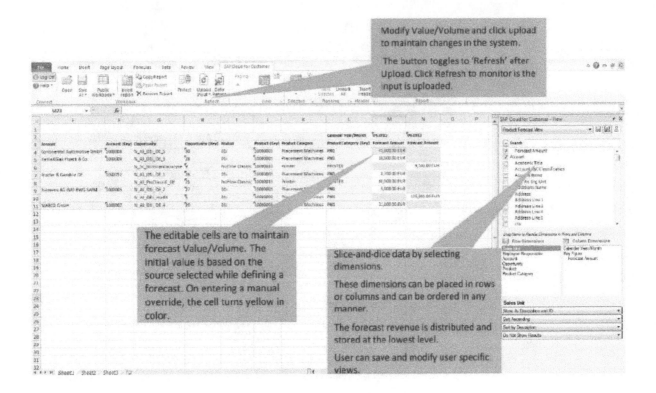

The editable cells are to maintain forecast Value/Volume. The initial value is based on the source selected while defining a forecast. On entering a manual override, the cell turns yellow in color.

Modify Value/Volume and click upload to maintain changes in the system.

The button toggles to 'Refresh' after Upload. Click Refresh to monitor is the input is uploaded.

Slice-and-dice data by selecting dimensions.

These dimensions can be placed in rows or columns and can be ordered in any manner.

The forecast revenue is distributed and stored at the lowest level.

User can save and modify user specific views.

84. **Which of the following cannot be done in Forecast Analytics?**

Please choose the correct answer.

a. Analyze data based on standard queries
b. Compare the Forecast with Pipeline and Target
c. Review Forecast variance between versions
d. None of the above

Answer: d

Explanation:

Forecast Analytics:

- Analyze data based on standard queries.
- Compare the Forecast with Pipeline and Target
- Review Forecast variance between versions
- Personalize these reports and add them to home screen

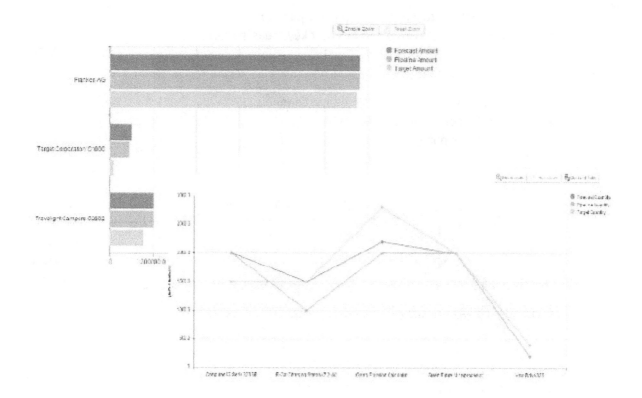

Visit Planning and Execution

85. **Which of the following are the benefits of Visit Planning and Execution?**

    Note: There are 2 correct answers to this question.

    a. More customer visits, fewer miles
    b. Sales route mapping
    c. Quick Appointment creation via iPad
    d. Easy creation of follow-up documents

    Answer: a, b

    Explanation:

    Visit Planning and Execution:

    Description:
    - Enable your field sales personnel to plan and record site visits and activities while on site at the account.

    Key Differentiators:

- Turn portables into a personal itinerary planner
- Perform surveys and audits to monitor key areas in stores

Benefits:
- Calendar management across multiple channels
- More customer visits, fewer miles
- Sales route mapping
- Ability to leverage Sales rep time working an area

Quick Appointment creation via iPad and Easy creation of follow-up documents are not the benefits of Visit Planning and Execution.

86. **Which of the following are the key differentiators of Visit Planning and Execution?**

Note: There are 2 correct answers to this question.

a. Collaboration support
b. Superior UI/UX
c. Turn portables into a personal itinerary planner
d. Perform surveys and audits to monitor key areas in stores

Answer: c, d

Explanation:

Visit Planning and Execution:

Description:
- Enable your field sales personnel to plan and record site visits and activities while on site at the account.

Key Differentiators:
- Turn portables into a personal itinerary planner
- Perform surveys and audits to monitor key areas in stores

Collaboration support and Superior UI/UX are not the key differentiators of Visit Planning and Execution

Benefits:

- Calendar management across multiple channels
- More customer visits, fewer miles
- Sales route mapping
- Ability to leverage Sales rep time working an area

87. **Surveys can be associated with which of the following?**

Note: There are 3 correct answers to this question.

a. Product
b. Visits
c. Tickets
d. Activities
e. Tasks

Answer: a, b, c

Explanation:

Survey Definition:

Surveys can be:
- Static
- Dynamic
- In matrix format

Surveys can be associated with:
- Product
- Visits
- Tickets

Easy Survey definition with support for creating questionnaires with standard question types.
- Multiple choice - multi-select
- Multiple choice - single-select
- Amount
- Quantity
- Text

88. **Which of the following statement(s) is/are true regarding Visit Planner?**

Please choose the correct answer.

a. Supported by map view and calendar on both browser and iPad
b. Search enabled by days since last visit
c. Both a and b
d. None of the above

Answer: c

Explanation:

Visit Planner:

- Supported by map view and calendar on both browser and iPad
- Search enabled by
  - Recommended frequency stores overdue for visits
  - Days since last visit
- Account 360 for more information
- Visits on the basis of proximity

89.   **Which of the following is NOT part of Visit Planning and Execution process?**

Please choose the correct answer.

a. Field Preparation
b. Field Execution
c. Headquarter Planning
d. Field Analytics
e. None of the above

Answer: e

Explanation:

Visit Planning and Execution – Process:

Below given is the process involved in Visit Planning and Execution:

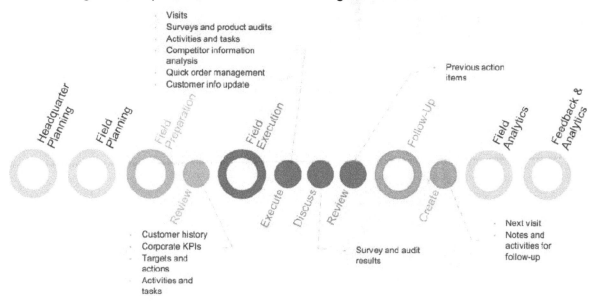

90.   **Which of the following statements are true regarding Visit Administration?**

Note: There are 2 correct answers to this question.

a. Enhanced account 360 with recommended visit frequency and visit history
b. Product lists to determine account specific product proposals
c. Easy quote creation with product lists
d. Check-in/check-out of visit

Answer: a, b

Explanation:

Below given is a detailed view of Visit Administration, Planning and Execution:

Visit Administration

✓ Easy survey definition

✓ Flexible activity planning and routing to enable definition and assignment of tasks and surveys to be performed in an account.

✓ Enhanced account 360 with recommended visit frequency and visit history.

✓ Product lists to determine account specific product proposals.

✓ Enhanced reporting on survey answers, visits, and visit tasks

Visit Planning

✓ Map based visit planning with integrated calendar view in browser and iPad.

✓ Rule based determination of recommended tasks and surveys from the activity plans and routine rules

✓ Select tasks and surveys to be completed in visit

Visit Execution

✓ Supported on browser and iPad and offline.

✓ Check-in / check-out of visit

✓ Add / complete tasks and surveys

✓ Ability to capture pictures to attach to survey results

✓ Create follow-up quotes, orders, opportunities, service tickets

✓ Easy quote creation with product lists

Fine Tuning

91. **Which of the following is/are some of the key responsibility/responsibilities for system administrators?**

Please choose the correct answer.

a. Configure of the system before Go-Live and after Go-Live
b. Maintain the user accounts
c. Adjust system parameters based on evolving company needs
d. Only a and b
e. a, b, and c

Answer: e

Explanation:

System administration refers to the configuration and maintenance of the SAP Cloud solution. The selected scope significantly simplifies the system setup by deploying the majority of the system settings.

Some of the key responsibilities for system administrators are:

- Configure of the system before Go-Live and after Go-Live
- Maintain the user accounts (additions, removals, authorizations, passwords, etc.)
- Adjust system parameters based on evolving company needs

- Handle incidents created by end users

92. **Which of the following statement(s) is/are true about Service Levels?**

    Please choose the correct answer.

    a. Service levels are used to specify the performance objectives for handling customer messages.
    b. Service levels can be used to measure the performance and the quality of your customer service.
    c. Both a and b
    d. None of the above

    Answer: c

    Explanation:

    Service levels are used to specify the performance objectives for handling customer messages, and based on this you can measure the performance and the quality of your customer service.

93. **Which of the following statements is/are true about Service Categories?**

    Please choose the correct answer.

    a. Service categories allow you to create and organize service categories and incident categories within service category catalogs.
    b. Service categories are used throughout the system to capture consistent information, to allow for reporting and benchmarking, and determining service level assignments.
    c. Both a and b
    d. None of the above

    Answer: c

    Explanation:

    Service categories allow you to create and organize service categories and incident categories within service category catalogs. These categories are used throughout the system to capture consistent information, to allow for reporting and benchmarking, and determining service level assignments.

94. **You can have how many active Service category catalog(s) per usage?**

    Please choose the correct answer.

    a. 1

b. 2
c. 3
d. 4

Answer: a

Explanation:

Service categories allow you to create and organize service categories and incident categories within service category catalogs. These categories are used throughout the system to capture consistent information, to allow for reporting and benchmarking, and determining service level assignments.

Catalogs are managed with versions. You can have only one active catalog per usage, for example for service requests, at any one time. This means that catalogs with overlapping periods and overlapping usages are not allowed.

Territory Management

95.   **Which of the following statement(s) is/are true?**

Please choose the correct answer.

a. In addition to using business roles for assigning general access to work centers and views, you also have the option of restricting read and write access for users to whom a business role is assigned.
b. Authorizations for certain views can be restricted either to employees or territories associated to the specific item in a view, or via assignment of the employee to an organizational unit.
c. Both a and b
d. None of the above

Answer: c

Explanation:

In addition to using business roles for assigning general access to work centers and views, you also have the option of restricting read and write access for users to whom a business role is assigned.

Authorizations for certain views can be restricted either to employees or territories associated to the specific item in a view, or via assignment of the employee to an organizational unit.

96.   **Sales target can be defined for which of the following dimensions?**

Note: There are 3 correct answers to this question.

a. Employee
b. Product
c. Territory

d. Task
e. Activity

Answer: a, b, c

Explanation:

Sales target can be defined for following dimensions:
- Employee
- Sales unit
- Account
- Product
- Product category
- Territory

Sales Target Plan: Sales Unit US (US1100):2020/01-2020/03

97.   **Which of the following statement(s) is/are true?**

Please choose the correct answer.

a. While editing sales plan if the dimensions are edited then the old Sales Plan data gets lost
b. Plan dimension will determine the level of granularity on which a plan can be created
c. Both a and b
d. None of the above

Answer: c

Explanation:

While editing sales plan if the dimensions are edited then the old Sales Plan data gets lost. Sales target can be defined for following dimensions:
- Employee
- Sales unit
- Account
- Product
- Product category
- Territory

Plan dimension will determine the level of granularity on which a plan can be created.

Account and Contact Management

98. **Which of the following is the key differentiator of Account 360 and Sales Intelligence?**

    Please choose the correct answer.

    a. Online and Offline capabilities
    b. Standard integration for pricing and currency conversion rates with ERP and CRM
    c. Easily run 'If-Then' analysis leveraging real time data in SAP Hybris Cloud for Sales
    d. Integrated access to SAP BW for advanced reporting

Answer: d

Explanation:

Account 360 and Sales Intelligence:

Description:
- Track your performance in real time and proactively drive the right opportunities to close. Forecast and perform what-if analysis to learn where to focus

Key Differentiators:
- Integrated access to SAP BW for advanced reporting

Benefits:
- Real time capabilities
- Easily configurable dashboards
- Scheduled report broadcasts
- Predictive Analytics

99.   **Which of the following are the benefits of Account 360 and Sales Intelligence?**

Note: There are 2 correct answers to this question.

a. Easily configurable dashboards
b. Predictive Analytics
c. Forecast based on multiple dimensions
d. Improved sales efficiency

Answer: a, b

Explanation:

Account 360 and Sales Intelligence:

Description:
- Track your performance in real time and proactively drive the right opportunities to close. Forecast and perform what-if analysis to learn where to focus

Key Differentiators:
- Integrated access to SAP BW for advanced reporting

Benefits:
- Real time capabilities
- Easily configurable dashboards
- Scheduled report broadcasts
- Predictive Analytics

100. **Once the account is added to SAP Hybris Cloud for Customer, you will see which of the following indicator next to the record?**

    Please choose the correct answer.

    a. A
    b. E
    c. D

d. N

Answer: a

Explanation:

D&B 360:

- Once the account is added to SAP Hybris Cloud for Customer, you will see an indicator [A] next to the record indicating this account already exists in SAP Hybris Cloud for Customer and the + icon is disabled, to avoid duplicates in SAP Hybris Cloud for Customer
- Account Detail view: You can open up an account, if it is already linked, you will see the snapshot from D&B 360

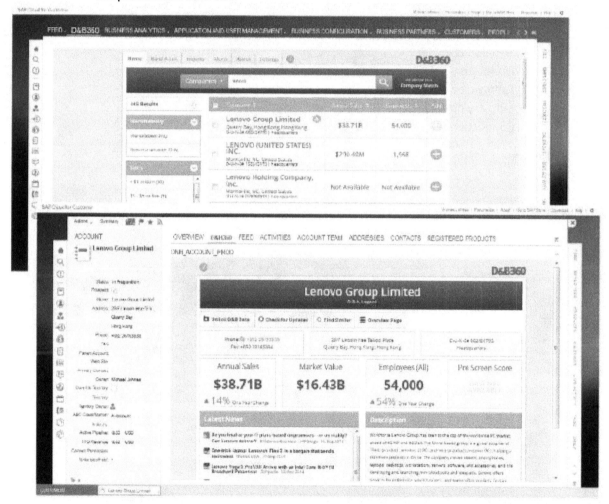

101. **Using the InsideView mashup within SAP Hybris Cloud for Sales, sales reps can get which of the following information about their accounts and contacts?**

Please choose the correct answer.

a. Company info
b. Family tree
c. Financial Forecasts
d. Only a and b
e. a, b, and c

Answer: d

Explanation:

Using the InsideView mashup within SAP Hybris Cloud for Sales, sales reps can get complete information about their accounts and contacts:

- Company info
- News alerts
- Social profiles
- Social buzz
- Financials
- Family tree
- Industry profiles
- Connections

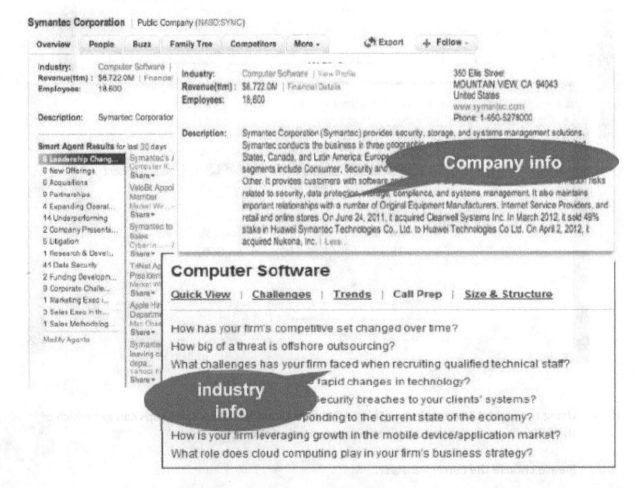

102.   **Using InsideView integration with SAP Hybris Cloud for Customer you can do which of the following?**

Please choose the correct answer.

a. Follow companies and people of interest
b. Learn their interests and issues
c. Engage in social conversations from within InsideView and SAP Hybris Cloud for Sales
d. Only a and b
e. a, b, and c

Answer: e

Explanation:

Using InsideView integration with SAP Hybris Cloud for Customer you can:
- Follow companies and people of interest
- Learn their interests and issues
- Build trust more quickly
- Engage in social conversations from within InsideView and SAP Hybris Cloud for Sales

103. **Which of the following statement(s) is/are true regarding Account 360?**

Please choose the correct answer.

a. Once Account 360 set-up is complete, the SAP On Premise system can communicate with SAP Hybris Cloud for Customer.
b. Account 360 set-up enables you to bring On Premise ERP/BI sales document data into the account details view in order to provide you with complete information about the sales transactions for the selected account
c. Both a and b
d. None of the above

Answer: c

Explanation:

Account 360:

Account 360 set-up enables you to bring On Premise ERP/BI sales document data into the account details view in order to provide you with complete information about the sales transactions for the selected account

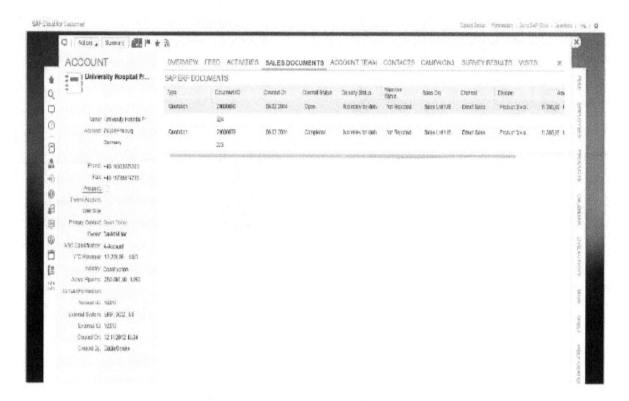

Once Account 360 set-up is complete, the SAP On Premise system can communicate with SAP Hybris Cloud for Customer.

When both halves of the bridge are in place, sales document information from your SAP On Premise system appears in SAP Hybris Cloud for Customer, providing a broader perspective to the sales reps.

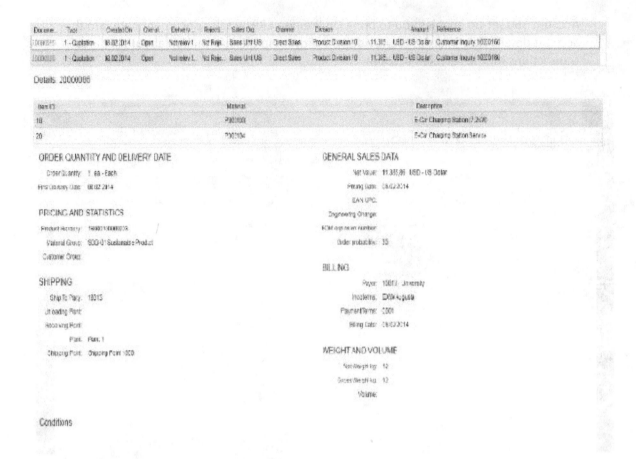

104. **Account 360 information in the Accounts view comes from which of the following system(s)?**

Note: There are 2 correct answers to this question.

a. SAP ERP
b. SAP BW
c. People Soft
d. Oracle

Answer: a, b

Explanation:

Account 360 information in the Accounts view comes from both SAP ERP and BW systems.
- The data in the Recent Orders tab is from ERP.
- The data in the Overview tab under the Revenue and Items Summary sections is from BW.

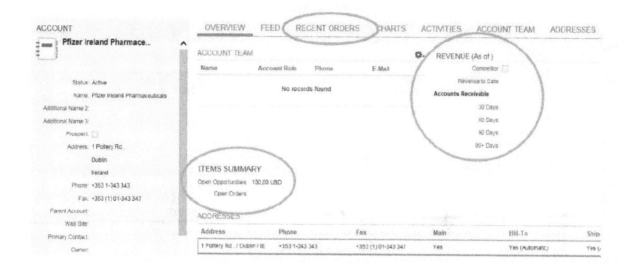

105. **Which of the following statement(s) is/are true regarding D&B 360?**

Please choose the correct answer.

a. Using the D&B 360 work center you can search and add accounts and contacts from the D&B 360 database
b. If key data points are missing for any account it will be shown as a flag
c. Both a and b
d. None of the above

Answer: c

Explanation:

Sales Intelligence – D&B 360:
- Using the D&B 360 work center you can search and add accounts and contacts from the D&B 360 database
- If key data points are missing for any account it will be shown as a flag, indicating data quality before you add such an account

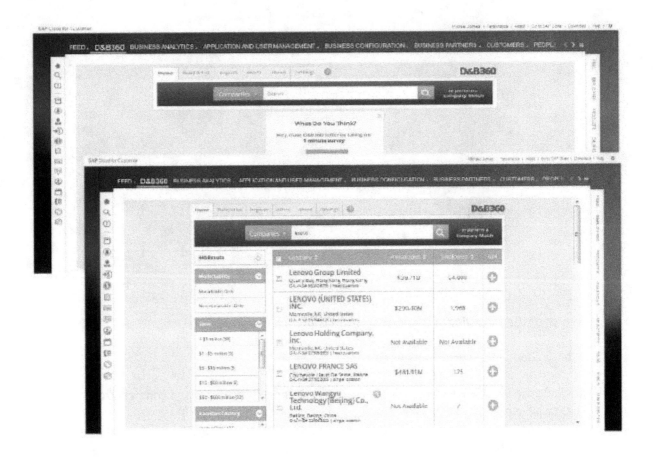

106.   **Which of the following statement(s) is/are true?**

Please choose the correct answer.

a. In D&B 360, you can mass select multiple accounts and click on 'Add selected' to add all of them
b. You can open up an account, if it is already linked, you will see the snapshot from D&B 360
c. Both a and b
d. None of the above

Answer: c

Explanation:

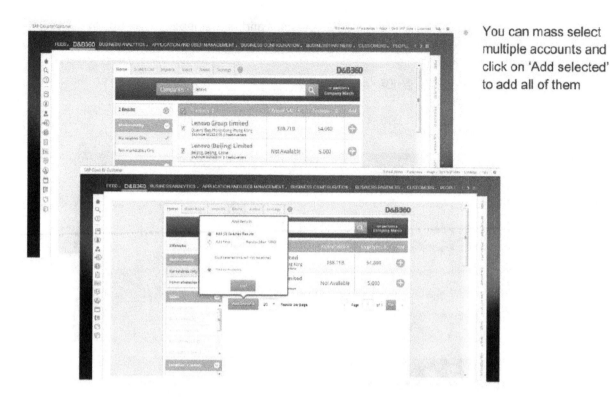

You can mass select multiple accounts and click on 'Add selected' to add all of them

- Once the account is added to SAP Hybris Cloud for Customer, you will see an indicator [A] next to the record indicating this account already exists in SAP Hybris Cloud for Customer and the + icon is disabled, to avoid duplicates in SAP Hybris Cloud for Customer

- Account Detail view: You can open up an account, if it is already linked, you will see the snapshot from D&B 360

107. **Which of the following statement(s) is/are true?**

Please choose the correct answer.

a. In D&B 360, you can also subscribe/unsubscribe to accounts for which you need these notifications or alerts via e-mail
b. In D&B 360, you can manage triggers for company alerts
c. Both a and b
d. None of the above

Answer: c

Explanation:
- Manage triggers for company alerts: Get notified about business triggers related to Market Share Info, Customer Wins or Losses, M&A and Spin-offs, Business Expansion and Exits, Product Initiatives, Management and Board Changes, Regulatory, Litigation

and Patents, Operating Activities, Partnerships and Agreements, Marketing Initiatives, Earnings & Dividends, Financing Activities, Bankruptcy

- You can also subscribe/unsubscribe to accounts for which you need these notifications or alerts via e-mail

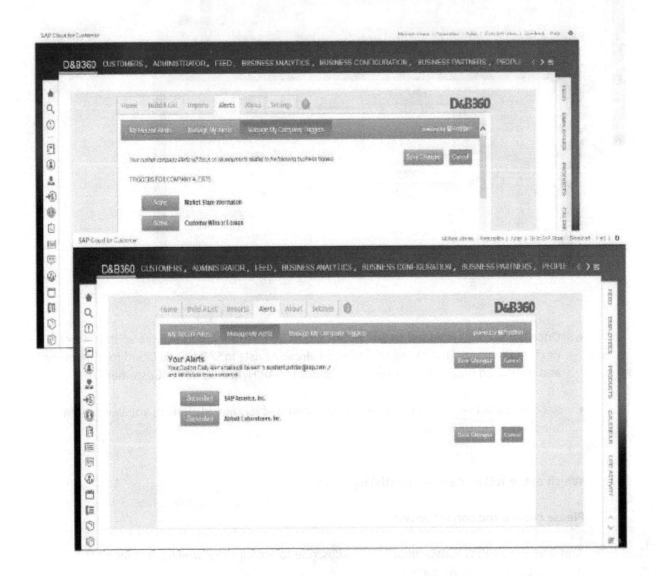

108.   **InsideView contains around how many company and contact profiles?**

Please choose the correct answer.

a. 1 million
b. 5 million
c. 10 million
d. 50 million

Answer: d

Explanation:

InsideView:

Get complete information of the company with essential Data, Insights, and Connections. The information in InsideView is constantly updated from 30,000 financial, media, and social sources. InsideView contains around 50 million company and contact profiles.

Implementation Basics

109.   **For SAP Cloud for Customer, which of the following toolkits are available?**

Note: There are 3 correct answers to this question.

a. SAP Cloud for Sales
b. SAP Cloud for Service
c. SAP Cloud for Social Engagement
d. SAP Cloud for Activity
e. SAP Cloud for Campaign

Answer: a, b, c

Explanation:

The Delivery Toolkit provides solution-specific workshops and tools which guide project team members through how to execute the methodology. The Delivery Toolkits are continually updated and increase customer value by making the best practices of many implementations available to the consultants.

For SAP Cloud for Customer, the following toolkits are available:

- SAP Cloud for Sales
- SAP Cloud for Service
- SAP Cloud for Social Engagement

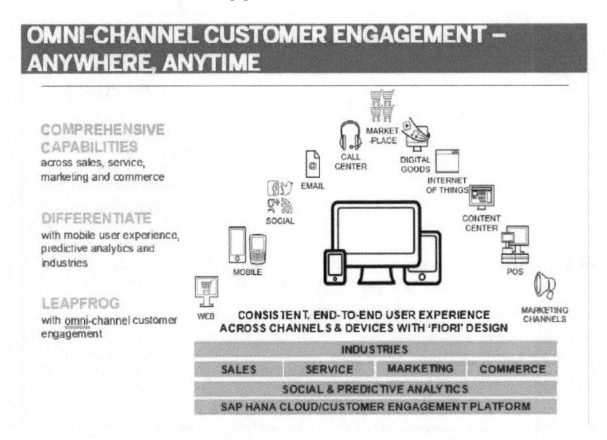

110. **SAP has developed SAP Launch, an implementation methodology for all SAP software-as-a-service (SaaS) that is based on best practices. There are how many phases in this methodology?**

Please choose the correct answer.

a. 3
b. 4
c. 5
d. 6

Answer: b

Explanation:

SAP has developed SAP Launch, an implementation methodology for all SAP software-as-a-service (SaaS) that is based on best practices. There are 4 phases in this methodology.

111. **The SAP Cloud for Customer Delivery Toolkits are comprised of which of the following?**

Please choose the correct answer.

a. Workshop presentations
b. Accelerators
c. Both a and b
d. None of the above

Answer: c

Explanation:

The SAP Cloud for Customer Delivery Toolkits are comprised of workshop presentations and accelerators. The delivery toolkits are maintained and used by a team of experienced field experts.

During projects, workshops are delivered based on the solution and the scope of the project. A workshop is an information sharing session focused on knowledge transfer to key users about the project and the solution. The workshops are designed to be conducted remotely. However, based on regional best practices or customer requirements, they may be delivered on-site.

The workshop materials are contained within the Delivery Toolkits and in addition to the standard workshops, there may be additional workshops (or accelerators) available for a specific solution.

112. **SAP Hosting Services has how many data centers in which tenants are established on systems?**

Please choose the correct answer.

a. 2
b. 3
c. 4
d. 5

Answer: b

Explanation:

SAP Hosting Services has three data centers in which tenants are established on systems.

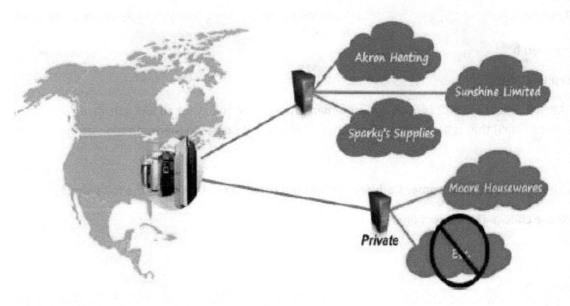

113. **There are how many versions of an implementation tenant landscape?**

    Please choose the correct answer.

    a. 1
    b. 2
    c. 3
    d. 4

    Answer: c

    Explanation:

    There are 3 versions of an implementation tenant landscape based on whether the customers has 2 or 3 tenants.

    Standard Implementation System Landscape with 2 Cloud Tenants

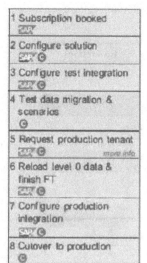

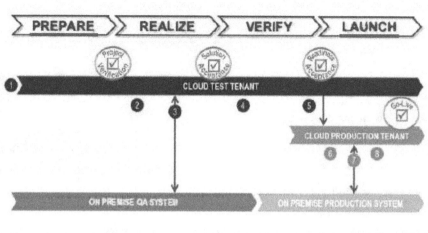

Exception Implementation System Landscape with 3 Cloud Tenants (Option A)

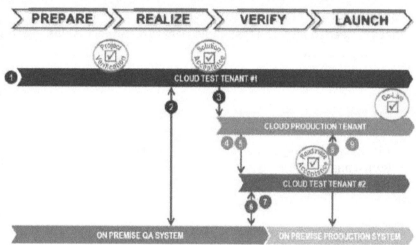

98

Exception Implementation System Landscape with 3 Cloud Tenants (Option B)

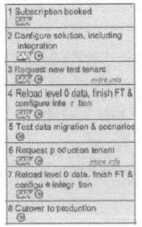
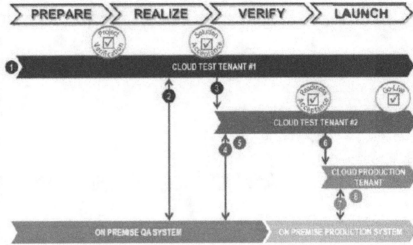

114. **Assume that SAP Cloud for Customer solution is live for productive use. Configuration changes that are needed after the first implementation project is closed can be handled in which of the following way(s)?**

Please choose the correct answer.

a. Minor changes can be made immediately
b. More complex changes must be made via a change project
c. Both a and b
d. None of the above

Answer: c

Explanation:

After the SAP Cloud for Customer solution is live for productive use, the First Implementation project should be closed in Business Configuration.

Configuration changes that are needed after the first implementation project is closed can be handled in one of two ways:

- Minor changes can be made immediately
- More complex changes must be made via a change project, which is a control that is introduced to mitigate risk to the live solution

115. **Copy of Source System is recommended for which of the following use?**

Please choose the correct answer.

a. For requesting production tenants

b. For data migration testing when initial test tenant cannot be used

c. Both a and b

d. None of the above

Answer: b

Explanation:

The table below outlines the recommended options for requesting new systems.

Data Source Used	Description	Recommended Use
Initial System (Copy Solution Profile)	• Can be system type of test or production • Source solution profile is copied and deployed • No data is copied • Relevant for initial implementation • Could be used after go-live but no merge back capability is possible	For requesting production tenants
Copy of Source System	• Can only be test system type • Triggers full copy (with solution profile and data) of a single source tenant • Can be relevant for initial implementation • Could be used after go-live but no merge back capability is possible • Source tenant must be	For data migration testing when initial test tenant cannot be used

	taken down for four hours outside of the normal maintenance window	
Copy of Source System (Copy Solution Profile)	• Can only be test system type • Source solution profile is copied and deployed (the change project solution profile can be selected) • Source data is copied (source tenant for solution profile can be different) • Relevant for initial implementation • Relevant for change project, including merge of solution profile back into production • Source tenant(s) must be taken down for four hours outside of the normal maintenance window	For requesting new change project test tenants ℹ *If a test tenant hosts an already copied/active change project, no other change project can be copied to this test tenant unless the change project is cancelled or completed*

116.   **Initial System (Copy Solution Profile) is recommended for which of the following use?**

Please choose the correct answer.

a. For requesting production tenants
b. For data migration testing when initial test tenant cannot be used
c. Both a and b
d. None of the above

Answer: a

Explanation:

The table below outlines the recommended options for requesting new systems.

101

Data Source Used	Description	Recommended Use
Initial System (Copy Solution Profile)	<ul><li>Can be system type of test or production</li><li>Source solution profile is copied and deployed</li><li>No data is copied</li><li>Relevant for initial implementation</li><li>Could be used after go-live but no merge back capability is possible</li></ul>	For requesting production tenants
Copy of Source System	<ul><li>Can only be test system type</li><li>Triggers full copy (with solution profile and data) of a single source tenant</li><li>Can be relevant for initial implementation</li><li>Could be used after go-live but no merge back capability is possible</li><li>Source tenant must be</li></ul>	For data migration testing when initial test tenant cannot be used

Copy of Source System (Copy Solution Profile)	• Can only be test system type • Source solution profile is copied and deployed (the change project solution profile can be selected) • Source data is copied (source tenant for solution profile can be different) • Relevant for initial implementation • Relevant for change project, including merge of solution profile back into production • Source tenant(s) must be taken down for four hours outside of the normal maintenance window	For requesting new change project test tenants *If a test tenant hosts an already copied/active change project, no other change project can be copied to this test tenant unless the change project is cancelled or completed*
	taken down for four hours outside of the normal maintenance window	

117. **When a solution profile is copied to a new production tenant, which of the following additional activities automatically occur?**

Please choose the correct answer.

a. Extension fields and screen layout adaptations made via key user tools are copied as long as there are no extension fields and/or screen layout adaptations already made in the new production tenant
b. Form adaptations are copied
c. Both a and b
d. None of the above

Answer: c

Explanation:

When a solution profile is copied to a new production tenant, the following additional activities automatically occur:

a. Extension fields and screen layout adaptations made via key user tools are copied as long as there are no extension fields and/or screen layout adaptations already made in the new production tenant

b. Form adaptations are copied

c. Level 0 master data is copied to a staging area where the user can choose to import the pre-populated data migration templates or ignore them.

118. **For approximately two weeks during which test tenants are upgraded and production tenants are not, which of the following are true?**

    Note: There are 2 correct answers to this question.

    a. Go-lives should be avoided
    b. Request new tenants
    c. Change projects can be merged from test to production
    d. Do not request termination of tenant

    Answer: a, d

    Explanation:

    For approximately two weeks during which test tenants are upgraded and production tenants are not:

    - Change projects CANNOT be merged from test to production
    - Go-lives should be avoided
    - Avoid applying SDK solutions
    - Do not request new tenants
    - Do not request termination of tenant

    Note that all previously requested restore points will no longer be available after the upgrade.

119. **There is/are how many UI framework(s) for SAP Cloud for Customer?**

    Please choose the correct answer.

    a. 1
    b. 2
    c. 3
    d. 4

Answer: b

Explanation:

There are two UI frameworks for SAP Cloud for Customer: Silverlight and HTML5.

General Screen Layout

The general screen layout is as follows:

Silverlight UI

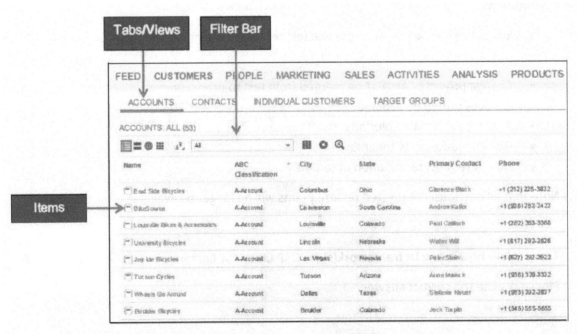

HTML5 UI

120. **All business user functions should be performed using which of the following client(s)?**

Please choose the correct answer.

a. Silverlight
b. HTML5
c. Both a and b
d. None of the above

Answer: b

Explanation:

The look and feel of the application is based on the settings and permissions assigned to you by your administrator.

The default client is HTML5 and all business user functions should be performed using that client.

The Silverlight client can only be accessed by administrators via the Adapt menu and must be used to perform most of the configuration and setup.

HTML5 UI

121. **Which of the following UI Element appear vertically on the right side of the screen and expand into the screen from the right?**

Please choose the correct answer.

a. Toolbar

b. Panes
c. Work Centers
d. Item

Answer: b

Explanation:

Screen Elements

UI Element	Description
Work Centers, Views, and Tabs	Work areas that are grouped by function.
Toolbar	A persistent vertical list of icons that appear on the left side of the screen, offering shortcuts for many of the basic functions, such as search and new.
Panes	Workspaces that appear vertically on the right side of the screen, and that expand into the screen from the right.
Filter Bar	An area of the screen that appears above a list of items and contains filtering and search tools.

122. **Which of the following UI Element is an object in the system that contains information and can be opened?**

Please choose the correct answer.

a. Toolbar
b. Panes
c. Work Centers
d. Item

Answer: d

Explanation:

Action Bar	A horizontal toolbar that appears on a list of items on the right side of the screen, above the filter bar. The action bar contains a New button and an actions icon that contains context-specific actions.
Item	An object in the system that contains information and can be opened. (i.e. Opportunity, Lead, Activity)
Quick View	An abbreviated item summary that appears when you rest the cursor on a linked item. The quick view allows limited editing functions.

123. **Which of the following statements are true?**

Note: There are 2 correct answers to this question.

a. In the SAP Cloud for Customer solution, scoping is the process of matching your individual business requirements to predefined solution capabilities using the business adaptation catalog.
b. The catalog structures all available capabilities for the solution into a hierarchy of business areas, packages, topics, and options.
c. During the scoping process, all of your decisions need not be stored in a unique solution proposal
d. Level 2 master data is copied to a staging area where the user can choose to import the pre-populated data migration templates or ignore them, when a solution profile is copied to a new production tenant

Answer: a, b

Explanation:

When a solution profile is copied to a new production tenant, the following additional activities automatically occur:

a. Extension fields and screen layout adaptations made via key user tools are copied as long as there are no extension fields and/or screen layout adaptations already made in the new production tenant

b. Form adaptations are copied

c. Level 0 master data is copied to a staging area where the user can choose to import the pre-populated data migration templates or ignore them.

In the SAP Cloud for Customer solution, scoping is the process of matching your individual business requirements to predefined solution capabilities using the business adaptation catalog.

The catalog structures all available capabilities for the solution into a hierarchy of business areas, packages, topics, and options.

SAP and its partners have already defined the technical system settings and the content needed to accommodate each element of the catalog and to support your requirements. This predefined content is based on industry-specific and country-specific best practices.

During the scoping process, all of your decisions are stored in a unique solution proposal. This document is available when you have finished scoping and contains detailed information about your scoping selections.

124. **Which of the following statement is true?**

Please choose the correct answer.

a. Most of the icons on the toolbar are associated with specific work centers and views
b. The toolbar is not available from every screen, so you have to navigate away from your current screen
c. There are no static tools that are available to all users
d. None of the above

Answer: c

Explanation:

The toolbar is available from every screen allowing you quick access to the tools you use most – without having to navigate away from your current screen.

Most of the icons on the toolbar are associated with specific work centers and views. So each user will only have access to the tools related to the work they do. For example, a customer service agent who is not assigned access to sales features won't have the icon for creating a new opportunity.

There are a few static tools that are available to all users like, Home, Search, and Notifications.

SAP Cloud for Customer

FEED   CUSTOMERS

FEED

Post an Upd:

All Updates

@Review Q1 Plan

Friday, August 22, 2

Sales Quote @8

Monday, August 18,

Toolbar Icons

125.   **SAP defines an issue as an unexpected behavior of the system that:**

Please choose the correct answer.

a. Interrupts the operation of a service
b. Reduces the quality of a service immediately or in the near future
c. Either a or b
d. None of the above

Answer: c

Explanation:

SAP defines an issue as an unexpected behavior of the system that:

- Interrupts the operation of a service, or
- Reduces the quality of a service immediately or in the near future

If a user encounters a problem in the application, he can search the knowledgebase for a solution. If no solution is available, then the user can report an incident to request help solving the problem.

The process flow for incident management:

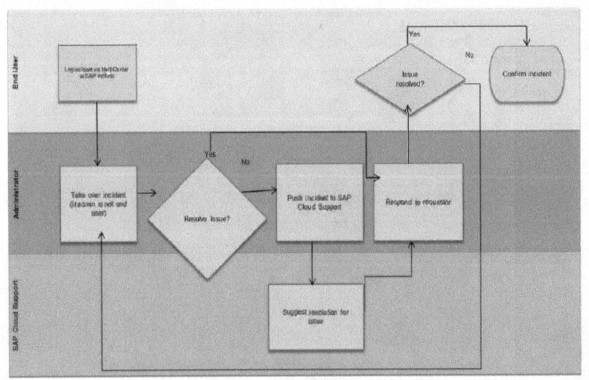

All communication occurs via SAP Cloud for Customer

126. **Which of the following statement(s) is/are true about Org Structure?**

Please choose the correct answer.

a. In order to successfully use and implement SAP Cloud for Customer, it is important that a customer's organization be set up correctly
b. Depending upon the size and complexity of the company, org structure setup may take several hours
c. Both a and b
d. None of the above

Answer: c

Explanation:

In order to successfully use and implement SAP Cloud for Customer, it is important that a customer's organization be set up correctly. You should work with the customer to map their org structure to the options provided in SAP Cloud for Customer.

111

In sales as well as in service, the most important organizational functions are the head of sales organization and the head of service organization. These properties define the top-most org unit of your sales or service hierarchy. This is where you will need to define all related master data relevant for your sales and service processes.

All other sales and service units must be placed below their head of organization counterparts. For this reason, there cannot be a head of sales organization placed above another head of sales organization. The same holds true for the head of service organization.

127. **Which of the following describe the role of the org unit in the structure?**

Please choose the correct answer.

a. Definitions
b. Addresses
c. Functions
d. Role Description

Answer: a

Explanation:

Definitions describe the role of the org unit in the structure. For example, company, business residence, or reporting line unit.

Functions reflect the business purpose of the org unit, like sales or service.

Addresses provide all address details for the org unit, including the e-mail address for outbound e-mails (used to respond to tickets, for example)

Notification Process

128. **Which of the following statement(s) is/are true?**

Please choose the correct answer.

a. Field updates automatically change the content of a field when the specified conditions are met.
b. Notifications are sent to users to inform them when items have changed under various conditions and to notify them of tasks to complete.
c. Both a and b
d. None of the above

Answer: c

Explanation:

Field updates automatically change the content of a field when the specified conditions are met.

Notifications are sent to users to inform them when items have changed under various conditions and to notify them of tasks to complete. If you set up e-mail notifications, they can also be sent to customers, for example when a ticket status has been changed.

As you define workflow rules, you specify basic data for each rule, the conditions under which the rule is invoked, and a field is updated, or a notification is sent, and in the case of a notification, the list of recipients.

129. **How many approval process/processes can be active for each transaction type?**

   Please choose the correct answer.

   a. 1
   b. 2
   c. 3
   d. 4

   Answer: a

   Explanation:

   Only one approval process can be active for each transaction type.

130. **By default, the approval process related to a business document in the SAP Cloud for Customer solution always consists of how many step(s)?**

   Please choose the correct answer.

   a. 1
   b. 2
   c. 3
   d. 4

   Answer: a

   Explanation:

   By default, the approval process related to a business document in the solution always consists of one step however you can define multi-step approval processes with different approvers and conditions.

   For example, a sales quote over a certain amount and for a specific product may require approval by both a manager and someone in the finance department. You may also require that conditions be incorporated into the approval processes, such as the amount that an approver is allowed to approve.

131. **You must have how many approval process/processes with an unlimited date?**

Please choose the correct answer.

a. 1
b. 2
c. 3
d. 4

Answer: a

Explanation:

Approval processes are only valid for a specified period of time because they are time-dependent. When you edit the validity of an approval process, the system displays the approval processes of the related business document that have not yet ended.

Note that the system allows neither gaps nor overlaps in the validity period of the approval processes.

Note that you must have one approval process with an unlimited end date; the approval process can have either the Active or Scheduled status.

132. **Which of the following statements are true?**

Note: There are 2 correct answers to this question.

a. Conditions within a group are OR conditions
b. Groups of conditions are linked by OR
c. Conditions within a group are AND conditions
d. Groups of conditions are linked by AND

Answer: b, c

Explanation:

Conditions are structured in groups. They offer a number of attributes depending on the related business document, such as the status or phase progress for an opportunity. These attributes can be used to define AND and OR conditions.

Conditions within a group are AND conditions. If all of them are met, the whole group of conditions is met, and approval is required

Groups of conditions are linked by OR. If all conditions within at least one of the groups are met, approval is required

133. **In a condition, you can select a compare operator and compare with which of the following?**

Please choose the correct answer.

a. A value
b. A field
c. Both a and b
d. None of the above

Answer: c

Explanation:

In a condition, you can select a compare operator and compare with the following:

A value

You can define a comparison using a value, such as a status

A field

You can define a comparison using a field in a business object

You can only compare similar fields in a condition, for example, you cannot compare a date field with a currency field. You can only compare field values that occur only once in the related business object, that is you cannot select a field value that has brackets next to it, such as product category [].

134. **SAP Cloud for Customer has which of the following native apps available that provide mobile access to the solution tenant?**

Note: There are 2 correct answers to this question.

a. SAP Cloud for Customer for Tablet
b. SAP Customer Insight for Tablet
c. SAP Cloud for Customer for iPhone
d. SAP Cloud for Customer for Android

Answer: c, d

Explanation:

SAP Cloud for Customer has the following native apps available that provide mobile access to the solution tenant:

- SAP Cloud for Customer for iPad
- SAP Customer Insight for iPad
- SAP Cloud for Customer for iPhone
- SAP Cloud for Customer for Android

In addition, the HTML5 client can be accessed from the browser on mobile devices like Android tablets.

135.   **Which of the following statement(s) is/are true?**

Please choose the correct answer.

a. Most of the core business features are available for use while offline
b. You need to set up your offline data preferences and then sync your data to your device to work in offline mode
c. When setting up your offline preferences, you can choose which type of data and how much of it to sync
d. Only a and b
e. a, b, and c

Answer: e

Explanation:

Most of the core business features are available for use while offline. You need to set up your offline data preferences and then sync your data to your device to work in offline mode. When setting up your offline preferences, you can choose which type of data and how much of it to sync.

To work with reports offline, report data needs to be synchronized separately simply by opening the report while online. This stores the data on your device and enables use while offline.

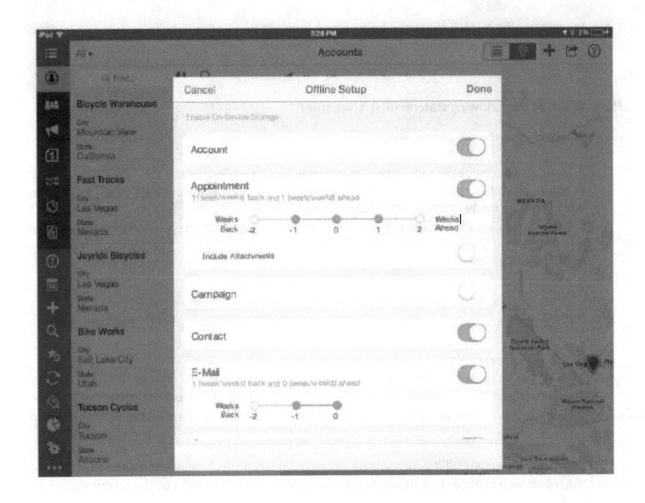

136. **Mashups can include which of the following?**

Note: There are 3 correct answers to this question.

a. Web searches
b. Company or industry business information
c. Online map searches
d. Sentiment Analysis
e. Forecast capabilities

Answer: a, b, c

Explanation:

Mashups can include the following:

- Web searches
- Company or industry business information
- Online map searches

137. **Which of the following are different Mashup types?**

   Note: There are 2 correct answers to this question.

   a. URL Mashup
   b. XML Mashup
   c. Excel Mashup
   d. Custom Mashup

   Answer: a, d

   Explanation:

   There are a few preconfigures mashups delivered with the solution as well as some additional preconfigured mashup web services that you can use to create mashups.

   Following are the four Mashup types:

   - URL Mashup
   - HTML Mashup
   - Data Mashup
   - Custom Mashup

138. **Which of the following Mashup combines and displays data from both internal and external sources?**

   Please choose the correct answer.

   a. URL Mashup
   b. HTML Mashup
   c. Data Mashup
   d. Custom Mashup

   Answer: c

   Explanation:

   A data mashup combines and displays data from both internal and external sources. To create a data mashup, an integrated authoring tool is used to transform or merge external Web services with internal business data using industry-standard Web service protocols.

   The Knowledge Base on the agent workspace in SAP Cloud for Service is an example of a data mashup.

139. **Which of the following is one that has been created as an add-on solution by SAP?**

   Please choose the correct answer.

a. URL Mashup

b. HTML Mashup

c. Data Mashup

d. Custom Mashup

Answer: d

Explanation:

A URL mashup sends data from the solution to the URL of an online service provider. The service provider uses the data, for example, to perform a search, and the results are displayed in a new browser window.

An HTML mashup is one that embeds an HTML or JavaScript based Web page directly on a screen.

A data mashup combines and displays data from both internal and external sources. To create a data mashup, an integrated authoring tool is used to transform or merge external Web services with internal business data using industry-standard Web service protocols.

A custom mashup is one that has been created as an add-on solution by SAP.

Reporting

140. **When implementing the Reporting in SAP Cloud for Customer solution, you need to determine which of the following?**

    Please choose the correct answer.

    a. Whether or not you want to assign reports to business roles in addition to the standard work center assignment.

    b. Whether or not you want to see real data rather than just test data when you're creating and reviewing your customer reports.

    c. Both a and b

    d. None of the above

    Answer: c

    Explanation:

    When implementing the solution, you need to determine whether or not you want to:

    - Assign reports to business roles in addition to the standard work center assignment.
    - See real data rather than just test data when you're creating and reviewing your customer reports.

    In order to enable these features, you have to make the associated settings in fine-tuning.

141. **Working with Standard Reports in SAP Cloud for Customer, Which of the following features are enabled by Advanced analysis pattern in the browser?**

Note: There are 3 correct answers to this question.

a. Drilldown
b. Manage tables
c. Defining cells
d. Defining Exceptions
e. Sorting

Answer: a, d, e

Explanation:

Advanced analysis pattern in the browser enables additional features such as

- Drilldown
- Sorting
- Defining exceptions and conditions
- Manage views etc.

142. **In SAP Cloud for Customer, which of the following can be performed with Standard Reports?**

Note: There are 3 correct answers to this question.

a. Microsoft excel based analysis and formatting of reports
b. Drilldown on Tablet
c. Mark reports as favorites
d. Enable reports on smart devices
e. Forecast analysis

Answer: a, c, d

Explanation:

In SAP Cloud for Customer, the following can be performed with Standard Reports:

- Microsoft excel based analysis and formatting of reports
- Drilldown on iPad
- Mark reports as favorites
- Enable reports on smart devices

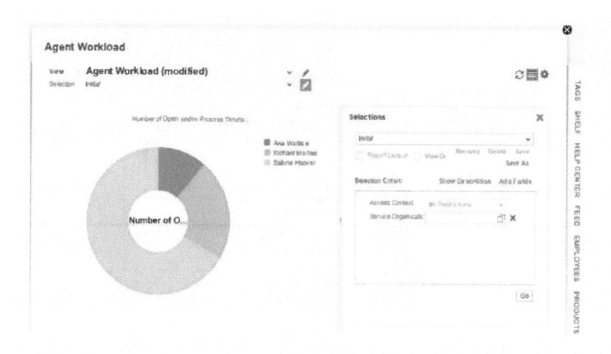

143. **Which of the following statements are true?**

Note: There are 2 correct answers to this question.

a. By simply using the log on option on the SAP Cloud for Customer ribbon tab, data can be refreshed to include any subsequent activity recorded in your SAP Cloud for Customer system
b. Data from reports inserted in Microsoft Excel cannot be referenced, mapped, and saved as part of a document
c. In SAP Cloud for Customer, not every user can modify a report to perform ad hoc analysis
d. Using the extensive and flexible business analytics features in SAP Cloud for Customer, you can easily create custom reports

Answer: a, d

Explanation:

Data from reports inserted in Microsoft Excel can be referenced, mapped, and saved as part of a document. By simply using the log on option on the SAP Cloud for Customer ribbon tab, data can be refreshed to include any subsequent activity recorded in your SAP Cloud for Customer system.

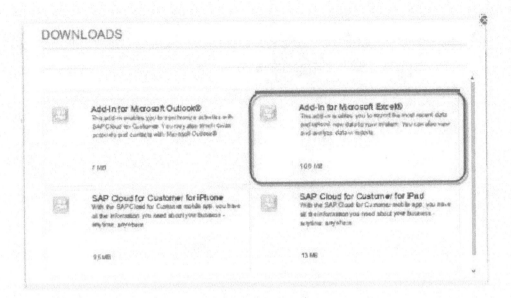

Any user can modify a report to perform ad hoc analysis and save their changes as a new view of the report. If you want to modify reports so that those changes apply to all users, you can make the changes as an administrator by creating a new view or copy of a report via Business Analytics.

Using the extensive and flexible business analytics features in SAP Cloud for Customer, you can easily create custom reports using the guided procedures and then control the visibility of these reports by assigning them only to specific work centers as well as individual business roles.

If you have defined custom fields in your solution, you can also add them to data sources or reports, your own or those delivered with the solution.

In addition, you can join or combine heterogeneous data sources, again your own or those delivered with the solution, as well as create custom calculated measures and comparison metrics.

144. **In SAP Cloud for Customer, the report creation process starts with selection of which of the following?**

Please choose the correct answer.

a. Data Source
b. Key Figures
c. Characteristics
d. Views

Answer: a

Explanation:

When you start the report creation process with the Report Wizard the first step is to select a data source. The solution ships with several pre-defined data sources. You can also create and edit your own data sources to suit your business requirements and processes and use your data sources for reporting.

145.   **Which of the following statement is true about calculated key figure?**

   Please choose the correct answer.

   a. A calculated key figure is a key figure determined using calculation rules or formulas
   b. A calculated key figure cannot be created from existing key figures in the selected data source.
   c. A calculated key figure is often created for comparison metrics
   d. None of the above

   Answer: a

   Explanation:

   Key figures are data items with numeric values and have an associated unit of measure or currency. Some examples are pipeline value, or tickets in queue. You can refine the data appearing in key figures by setting up restricted or calculated key figures.

   -    A calculated key figure is a key figure determined using calculation rules or formulas. You can create a calculated key figure from existing key figures in the selected data source.

   Key figures are data items with numeric values and have an associated unit of measure or currency. Some examples are pipeline value, or tickets in queue. You can refine the data appearing in key figures by setting up restricted or calculated key figures.

   -    A restricted key figure is a key figure restricted to a specified characteristic value, and is often created for comparison metrics

146.   **You set properties to define additional behavior for a specific characteristic through which of the following?**

   Note: There are 3 correct answers to this question.

   a. Display Settings
   b. Value Selections
   c. Hierarchy Settings
   d. Exception Settings
   e. Conditional Formatting

   Answer: a, b, c

   Explanation:

You set properties to define additional behavior for a specific characteristic.

- **Display Settings**

  Defines how the characteristic appears and is used in the report.

- **Value Selections**

  Add restrictions to the characteristic values that appear in the report.

- **Hierarchy Settings**

  Define how any hierarchical data associated with the characteristic is used in the report. For example, display the customer characteristic by location.

147. **You assign reports to which of the following in order to make them available for users?**

     Please choose the correct answer.

     a. Work centers
     b. Roles
     c. Both a and b
     d. None of the above

     Answer: c

     Explanation:

     You assign reports to specific work centers and roles in order to make them available for users.

     Work Centers

     You assign a report to a work center when you create or edit a report. A report must be assigned to a work center to be available to users.

     Roles

     If you have enabled the assignment of reports to roles in the fine tuning activity: Administrator Analytics – Settings, then you can also assign reports to roles. This restricts, by role, which users can view the report on the assigned work center.

148. **Which of the following statement is true about Views?**

     Please choose the correct answer.

     a. Even after you assign a report to a work center, you cannot select the view which appears in the end user reports list
     b. Even after you create a view, you cannot define conditions and exceptions for key figures
     c. You create a view by choosing key figures and characteristics for columns and rows in a table, then selecting a chart type to best represent that data

d. None of the above

Answer: c

Explanation:

Views enable you to set up one or more variations on which key figures and characteristics appear in the report and the type of chart that appears for the report. Once you assign a report to a work center, you can select the view which appears in the end user reports list.

You create a view by choosing key figures and characteristics for columns and rows in a table, then selecting a chart type to best represent that data. When you create a view you can also define conditions and exceptions for key figures that alter how your data is presented based on rules and thresholds.

149. **Which of the following can be used to set a threshold beyond which the data display is altered to display an alert indicator?**

    Please choose the correct answer.

    a. Conditions
    b. Exceptions
    c. Both a and b
    d. None of the above

    Answer: b

    Explanation:

    When you create a view you can also define conditions and exceptions for key figures that alter how your data is presented based on rules and thresholds.

    Conditions

    Create a condition to limit the data shown to that which fits the defined rules.

    Exceptions

    Set a threshold beyond which the data display is altered to display an alert indicator.

150. **SAP Cloud for Customer delivers several interactive dashboards that provide which of the following?**

    Please choose the correct answer.

    a. In-place interactivity and drilldown
    b. Advanced analysis on iPad

c. Single set-up for browser and iPad
d. Only a and b
e. a, b, and c

Answer: e

Explanation:

SAP Cloud for Customer delivers several interactive dashboards that provide you with a big picture of your data in real-time. You can zoom in by selecting a chart element, or by selecting specific characteristics, and applying filters.

Dashboards provide:

- In-place interactivity and drilldown
- Advanced analysis on iPad
- Single set-up for browser and iPad
- Easy, guided wizard to create and publish

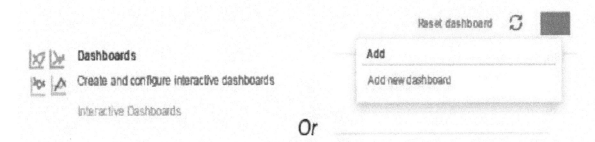